GOD IS ALIVE!

GOD IS ALIVE!

Bibliografische Information der Deutschen Nationalbibliothek:
Die Deutsche Nationalbibliothek verzeichnet diese Publikation in der
Deutschen Nationalbibliografie; detaillierte bibliografische Daten sind
im Internet über dnb.dnb.de abrufbar.

Bibliographic information from the German National Library:
The German National Library lists this publication in the German
National Bibliography; detailed bibliographic data is available on the
Internet at dnb.dnb.de.

Inhalt, Lektorat, Cover, Illustrationen, Gestaltung:
Content, editing, cover, illustrations, design:
© WITHJESUS.ME
Herstellung und Verlag: BoD – Books on Demand, Norderstedt
Manufacturing and Publishing: BoD – Books on Demand, Norderstedt
ISBN 978-3-7583-1379-0

Table of contents

6

To this book the perfect addition is the Bible
as well as the book "Believing? Knowing!" by the WithJesus-Team

Dear readers,

please don't borrow this book, please buy it –

With the purchase of this book, you support the charitable work of the WithJesus-Team.

For a low purchase price you get 150 pages of great, uplifting and exciting background information ...

... AND you do your part in helping to create affordable housing for people in need.

If you bought this book: Thank you!!!

The WithJesus-Team wishes you God's blessings

0.0 Preface?
Unnecessary!

0.1 No Time To Talk Around

Dear Sirs and Madams,

Lifetime is precious, so we're getting straight to the point:

With this book we, the WithJesus-Team, want to convey the most encouraging message in the world to you. We also want to help alleviate the suffering in this world as well as answer the same old, frequently asked questions.

With consistent, scientifically proven facts.

The brilliant journalist Herbert Völker and his friend, racing driver Niki Lauda, once very aptly lamented "... the ever increasing realization of the pointlessness of talking around" in Lauda's biography.

Not a day, not a minute comes back – money can be earned again if lost ... but not time. Therefore, the following is important:

Before you begin reading, *please* ask God in a brief prayer to help you understand the content of this book with the help of the Holy Spirit. *Now, please.* The authors of this book do realize that this may not make any sense to you. But rest assured that its meaning will be explained in this book!

If you wish that God helps you to have your life develop in unimaginable ways, leading to increased freedom and fulfilment then read this book.

Yeeees, we know the effects such words could have on some readers. Before we, the authors of the WithJesus-Team, became Christians we also could only smile faintly, while shaking our heads listening to such words.

This book contains the most valuable, scientifically proven information that a person can get. Therefore ...

0.2 ... read first: How Should This Book Be Read?

Now.

1.0 What Is the Most Important Question Of Humanity?

I.I Maybe: How Can I Have More Sex?

Please understand this somewhat non-conformist beginning of our book, but it seems that a large part of humanity only seems to focus on this one question: How can I have more sex?

In chapter 6.2 we read that sex is not at all forbidden by God. On the contrary it is His beautiful present for us.

After a certain age, however, one tends to become less concerned with the troubling question of potency :-) and instead, is able to think more freely – and ask other questions. Maybe this one?

I.2 Or: How Can I Have More Money?

In later years, people tend to think more intensively about the issues of securing one's existence, fulfilling one's wishes, preparing for the years of old age, leaving inheritance behind for one's children, or even engaging in charitable work. In this phase of life these questions become significantly more important than the question of sex.

In turn, even older people can't work energetically anymore. They start wishing for peace within the family, quiet, harmony, and a relaxed retirement much more than for money.

The elderly have reached a powerful realization that is only hardly understood by young people: Life can be over soon or maybe even at any moment.

What comes next?

We conclude that the question of money can't be the most important one either.

Wouldn't the most important question for mankind then be:

I.3 Does God Exist?
Then, What Would Be the Consequences?
Which God Is It?
How Can I Recognize Him?

If God really existed, ...

... then maybe there is life after death, and I will see my deceased relatives and friends again?

Do heaven, paradise and hell exist?
Where do I end up after death? Does God hear me when I pray?

If there was a God, then all social, ethical, moral resolutions of humans would have a deeper meaning.

Because in every religion there is a certain set of rules which somehow rewards "good people" and causes "bad people" to feel the consequences of their actions.

But which or whose God could it be?

How can one know that he is "the one God"?
That would also mean that all other religions whose God he *wouldn't* be, would be an illusion ..

If God were to exist, then another question could be answered, namely that about the meaning of life.

Regardless of all personal opinions, impressions and experiences, which are understandable for all logically thinking humans:

The WithJesus-Team is absolutely convinced to have found evidence of the existence of *the one* God.

2.0 God Is Alive! Sapere Aude! Consistent Facts = More Than "Truth"! Why It Can Only Be the God of the Bible

2.I What Does "Sapere Aude" Mean? What We Shouldn't Do Now

Sapere Aude is a famous exhortation by the Latin poet **Horace** (65-8 BC) and means something like: "dare to be wise".
Emmanuel Kant, philosopher, cited it as his legendary motto in 1784 of the **Enlightenment:** "Enlightenment is man's release from his self-incurred tutelage – Sapere aude! Have courage to use your own reason!" **Use your own reason, or put more simply, your brain? Yes! That's what we want to do here!**

What we shouldn't do now – Beware of self-deception:
One can arrive at subjective impressions and experiences, which are falsely deemed to have spiritual orgins in every religion, in meditations, in spiritualistic sessions or through "masters" of random faith groups, sects – **This is *not* we are looking for!**

We also want to look for more than opinions or even "the truth" – a term that is used abusively and excessively too often. We want to ***work scientifically*** and are looking for the ***consistent facts*** as evidence for the living God.

Dear readers, please forget all prejudice you may have towards the Bible, regardless of whether they stem from unfortunate situations, subtle influences or because you were bored in church as a child.

Please, **as Emmanuel Kant urges us, have the courage to let yourself be refreshed anew by the Bible and this booklet in front of you, which has the greatest adventure in the universe ready: *just for you.***

2.2 God Is Alive - Scientific Evidence - The Greatest and Most Important Miracle of Your Life!

With all due respect: if the following lines don't touch you, dear readers, then you have not understood the message: **The greatest good news of the world is about to come here and now in the upcoming lines.**
Please read them carefully, paying close attention to them:

The Bible is the only proven supernatural book in the world.
(Except for a few books by prophets, but **all** of them strangely were Jews or Christians). **Now let's look at them in a logical order:**
1.) In the Bible it is written that prophets received information about *specific* events in the future, otherwise unknown by them.
These pieces of information were, for example about the fate of cities, kings, peoples, the outcome of wars and much more.
The prophets got this information about the events *before* the events took place – that is historically and logically provable.
2.) This information, namely announcements was not known previously to them.
3.) *All* of these announcements came true – It is proven that they came true *after* the prophets had received them. They came true even when the prophets had considered them to be completely unlikely to ever happen.
4.) These biblical announcements must have a kind of "sender" who
5.) *must be alive,* because something "dead" can't make any announcements.
6.) The sender must be independent from our spatial and temporal structures since this person can look into the future.
7.) The sender must like us somehow, otherwise they wouldn't notify us about anything. And they offer us eternal life and much more.

This description perfectly fits *the* God the Bible speaks of and whose "factuality" is proven here, because ...
... these conclusions are called in scientific work (a defined term) as a "consistent fact", and ...
... we have zero intentions to fake an illusion for neither you, dear readers, nor ourselves. This is *more than truth:*

- **Conclusion 1/3: Here, on this book page, we have found that the Bible proves: GOD IS ALIVE.**

Only the Bible predicts binding concrete events, which were proven to have taken place in actuality afterwards: Almost exactly 6408 prophecies, of which at the time 3268 have come true[1]. **Hit rate: 100 percent.** The remaining prophecies in the Bible are announced for the future – therefore we can expect that they, too, will 100% will come true. So, the Bible is inspired *supernaturally,* by a being, which is "above our own nature", beyond our dimensions, our spatial and temporal structures. No other "user manual for a religion" (©WithJesus :-)) can do that. **Therefore, the Bible is** *at least* **the most likely and most reliable proof of the existence of a God.**

With that the assertion, "Christians believe in God because of fear of transience, eternity" etc., which is believed by many people, **is refuted,** since the arguments of this chapter are scientifically verifiable facts.

Was Jesus the Son of God? About **300 Bible prophecies announce not only the coming and life of Jesus** with precise descriptions (hundreds of years before Jesus was born!), but also that Jesus is the Son of God and our Saviour. **Hit rate: also 100%.** It is even confirmed by Roman historians, among others! *Everyone,* who follows Jesus, is His child (see John 1,12-13), but Jesus is *God's very special child – His Son.*
• **Conclusion 2/3: here, on this page of this book, we have found: JESUS IS THE SON OF THE GOD OF THE BIBLE and our Redeemer.**

The facts of this chapter prove: God conveys himself only through the Bible and the Jews, **since the Bible was exclusively written by the Jews.** Although the Jews are the "people of God" in the Bible, did they create a memorial for themselves with the Bible or did they gain an advantage from it? No! For the Jews describe with an astonishing honesty all of their missteps, their unfaithfulness, their apostasy from God and the resulting consequences. They, however, also describe the "happy ending" for *all* humanity!

• **Conclusio 3/3: This is why the Bible is the most credible book in the world.**

Biblical prophecies speak about the future, so that all people may prepare themselves accordingly and also receive immense blessings. Counterargument:

"But, but the Bible was written by people!" Right.
But God himself dictated it! See page 13, points 1 to 7.

---

1 Gitt, Dr. Werner, "Questions – that are asked again and again", Christian literature dissemination, Bielefeld 1998, p. 29. "At the time" means: spring 2023

2.3 God Sees and Hears You When You Pray, You Can Hear Him and Ask for Help, Prayer Helps — Not Everything Is Predetermined!

Before we get into the miracle of Bible prophecy, here's a preliminary, important information for you: **When you pray, you will benefit from it. And praying is very easy:** Jesus explains this in

Matthew 6,6f: *"But when you pray, go into your room, close the door and pray to your Father, who is unseen. Then your Father, who sees what is done in secret, will reward you. And when you pray, do not keep on babbling like pagans, for they think they will be heard because of their many words. Do not be like them, for your Father knows what you need before you ask him."*

Aha – **God knows, before we ask Him for something we need – not just what we want. These two things are often not the same.**

Thank God we don't need strange garments in Christianity, thousands of incense sticks, nor do we have to through ourselves on the ground countless times, twirl, chant, hum or perform other strange rituals.

When we pray we can meet the God of the Bible as honestly as a child meets its loving parents.

Think of this book an adventurous journey. It doesn't make sense to keep listening to the rumours or to get stuck trusting self-deception or myths. Whoever wants to find the Ark of the Covenant like this famous movie archaeologist with his hat and his whip, needs to get up, gather **facts,** inquire, investigate and follow up on clues.

Just like the prophets of the Bible, Christians have heard God speak, including the authors of this book! You can too – just ask God for it.

To be explained in further detail shortly.

But let's allow God speak for a moment! How does introduce himself to someone? Just like He answers Moses' question about name of God, by speaking through the burning bush for example:

Exodus 3,14: *"God said to Moses: 'I am who I am! This is what you are to say to the Israelites: I am has sent me to you'."*

It doesn't get any clearer than this:

Gott describes himself as the "I am who I am!"

The "Indescribable" describes himself, and Moses speaks to Him ...

Can you talk to God or even see Him? One of the most beautiful passages in the Bible:

The Bible says people can talk to God. This is unbelievable! Linked to that, here is one of the loveliest and most beautiful passages in the Bible, namely **Exodus 33,11:** *"And the Lord would speak to Moses face to face, **as one speaks to a friend** ..."*

When the authors of the WithJesus-Team first read these words for the first time they believed that this must be some loose description of a bible passage, which aims to make the content of the Bible more accessible to teenagers. However, these words are *exactly* what the Bible says.
A human being and God talked like good old friends – isn't that great?
To experience *just that* is a goal to which one should devote one's life!
If it worked then, why not today? Please imagine that it actually worked:
To speak with God personally!
Then you experience personally that ... God is alive!

But what does God's voice sound like? A voice like thunder, an echoing bass, or a the rushing Nigara Falls? No.

The Bible tells us how God spoke to His prophet Elijah, namely in
1 Kings 19,11: *"The Lord said 'Go out and stand on the mountain in the presence of the Lord, for the Lord is about to pass by.' Then a great and powerful wind tore the mountains apart and shattered the rocks before the Lord, but the Lord was not in the wind. After the wind there was an earthquake, but the Lord was not in the earthquake. After the earthquake came a fire, but the Lord was not in the fire. And after the fire came a **gentle whisper**. When Elijah heard it, he pulled his cloak over his face and went out and stood at the mouth of the cave. Then a voice said to him, ,'What are you doing here, Elijah?'"*
This is how God's voice is described and this is how many Christians hear Him: No storm, no earthquake, no fire, but instead a gentle wind, described as a "whispering" in some bible translations. Many Christians hear this voice like a "whispering in the head". But it is exactly in this voice that they feel unbelievable completeness and a "restfulness" no human in this world can portray.

Here is one of countless examples that actually happened: A young member of our team who decided to follow Jesus after a turbulent life wrote a letter to a former girl friend in which he asked for forgiveness. He wanted to cite a particular bible passage but didn't know the Bible well enough yet and looked for it to no avail .... At some point he noticed that he had heard a whisper the whole time inside: "Luke 10 ... Luke 10 ...". The young man first thought that these were his own thoughts, but then he checked Luke 10 in his Bible – and there was exactly the passage he was looking for! He couldn't have known that back then since he had only just begun studying the Bible. This is one proof for the "factuality" of God! The young man froze in humility and gratitude because of the love of God and His personal devotion to him, the "baby Christian"!

If the old prophets of the Bible heard God's voice and were able to speak with God, just like "with an old friend", like Moses, then you, dear readers, can do the same! God is looking forward to you!

Of course, it is possible that you are influenced by your own thoughts. But that is normal. This is precisely the **big challenge** that we learn to **"separate the wheat from the chaff"**: How far can we put aside our ego, our wishes and worries for once, for once let the world be the world and just approach God with trust? This can be accomplished best when we continually seek fellowship with God and that is what Gott wishes too.

For this, the term **"quiet time"** is widely used in Christianity, which means that you turn off your TV, your computer, your smartphone and instead sit down at a quiet place, relax not thinking about anything else than enjoying God's presence and finally hearing if He has anything to say. In this way God can help us to lead a fulfilled life in the midst of all the distractions in a fallen creation. (More on this will follow soon on p.20).
And with time you will learn to recognize this voice.

And, to reiterate, this voice is not from any "collective subconscious", from no "spiritual ether" whatsoever or from "the infinite loving energy" – all of these are explanatory models of Esotericists or of Occultists. For we humans are much more than organic mechanisms, we are living people, alive in the *emotional, the creative and the individual sense.*

The Bible describes us humans as creatures created in God's image, so it can only be the *emotional, creative and individual* God of the Bible who *personally* created us. God personally – literally *in person.*

So that He can be glorified God sometimes tells us things that we can't know, which then turn out to be true – that is, genuine prophecies. Through this He reveals himself to us and at the same time confirms His supernaturality and his existence.

*Because only a **living being** beyond our dimension of space and time was able to dictate pieces of information about the future to the prophets, **ALL of which came true!*** More on this topic in chapter 3.3.

Moreover, a nature, a universe, which brings forth individual and creative beings, must have the ability of individuality and creativity *within itself*. How could a dead universe "create" living creatures? How could a stone turn into a bird? From a metaphysical perspective, that would be impossible. More on this in chapter 2.6.

But what about seeing? Can you see God too?

God is like a being from another dimension, which is why we can't see Him with our "carnal" eyes in our "physical" dimension. God is salvation and this world is not (yet) healed, so He can't show himself to us in the same way as a three-dimensional cube doesn't fit into a two-dimensional plane: At the sight of Him our mortal bodies would simply be torn away – please excuse the dramatic imagery! When Moses one day asked God *"Let me see Your glory!"*
God explained it to Moses in the following way, found in
Exodus 33,20: *"'But,' He said, 'you cannot see my face, for no one may see me and live.'"*
But two verses further, God gives Moses a look: *"When my glory passes by, I will put you in a cleft in the rock and cover you with my hand until I have passed by. Then I will remove my hand and you will see may back; but my face must not be seen."*
God protects Moses from His own sight! Only when we are with Him in paradise are we allowed to see God personally. This is what John writes in
1. John 3,2: *"Dear friends, now we are children of God ... But we know that when Christ appears, we shall be like him; **for we shall see him as he is.**"*

Read how a child, which was not under the influence, close with the WithJesus-Team could briefly see God in paradise in chapter 2.7!
We can neither completely grasp God spiritually nor see him completely, especially not with our earthly eyes. That's why He doesn't want us to try and depict

him in pictures and statues. Still, we are already (!) saturated with God, there is nothing else apart from Him as Paul tells us in

Acts 17,28: *"For in him we live and move and have our being."*

Please see illustration 1 on this page.

It is God's deepest wish that we turn to him in our own free will!

This is why God *woos* us in many places of the Bible, wanting to gain our love and trust. Here are two of these passages:

Isaiah 55,6-7: *"Seek the Lord while he may be found: call on him while he is near. Let the wicked forsake their ways and the unrighteous their thoughts. Let them turn to the Lord, and he will have mercy on them, and to our God, for he will freely pardon!"*

And **Jesus** gives us His **personal recommendation** in

Luke 11,9: *"So I say to you: Ask and it will be given to you; seek and you will find; knock and the door will be opened to you."*

God cares about us, He wants to lead us into His whole dimension, meaning His kingdom of peace, of love. He woos us, He wants to help us, He has mercy on us and He wishes to have a personal relationship with us. Yes, that's possible! You can put it any way you want, but one thing is certain: God is like a caring father for His beloved children – and that's us!

Illustration 1:

Do you see the human figure in the font? It shows how God flows through everything, how we humans are completely interwoven with God.

This idea is from the: WithJesus-Team, copying prohibited, thank you.

Nothing is outside of God, and this is how He can give us His ideas, literally inspire us with the Holy Spirit, supernaturally heal us from diseases. We can hear Him, and He can help us in life.

We only need to let Him, by asking Him – in our own, informal language, just like a child asks its parents.

℗©**WITH JESUS**®

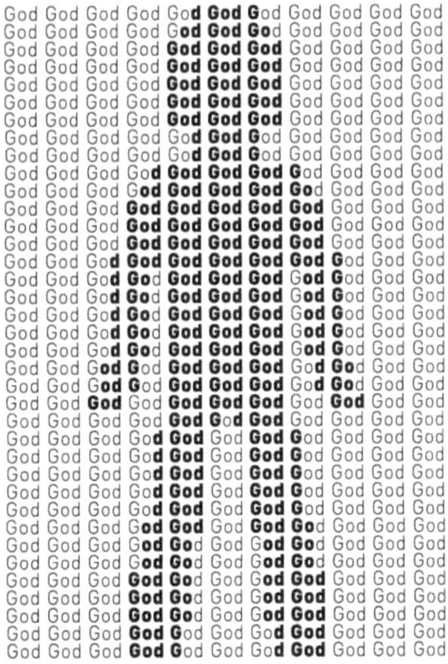

19

How to Hear God:

"Quiet time" is an established term for many Christians: Our human brains are filled to the brim with media overload, worries, desires. Then how can you hear God? Plan a few minutes of "quiet time" every day, push away your thoughts, set the mood by reading a few verses in the Bible (more information about that in chapter 2.8) or by listening to a worship song and finally have fellowship with God in a relaxed, friendly manner. Thank God for everything you can think of – this is how many people realize how God provides for them. You can also always ask Him for something, for example, that He tells you something. Close your eyes and listen ... no, not with your "carnal" ears. Instead, it's similar to when you have the voice of a loved one in your memories – then, you also have their sound "in your ear".

Dreams: When the human mind, which is often "blocked" by a multitude of thoughts throughout the day, can finally rest in sleep, then God's words can finally come through to us. Sometimes God himself hides behind a person in a dream and gives us words of help, of consolation, warnings, confirmations, or announcements.

Impressions, "Images": These terms, too, are established in Christianity. Often Christians can, in their thoughts, get a picture, some ideas, a passage from the Bible (with which God wants to show us something), a helpful word from God for yourself or other people. This can, for example, happen during "quiet time". **Even if it doesn't happen right away, God will answer you.**

Summary of this chapter:
1) God is alive
2) God hears us
3) God sees us
4) God knows how we are doing and what we really need
5) God is happy when we come to Him. We can talk to Him like with a friend ... and He talks to us too.
6) With the Bible God gave us His tips on how we can live a blessed and sacred life, combined with unfolded talents.
7) God loves us!
John 10,27: *"My sheep listen to my voice; I know them, and them follow me."*
This is a quote from Jesus – in one word: *God can be experienced!*

2.4 Prayer Helps — NOT Everything Is Predetermined!

Of course, praying helps! Whenever we pray for something and as a result God answers it by healing us, helping us, solving problems, we can't be sure if the final result would've been different without prayer. But whenever something turns out badly without us having prayed beforehand we know that we should've prayed about it! This is because prayer doesn't do any harm, it can only help – logically. Also: **Gott and Jesus recommend prayer repeatedly!**
Matthew 18,19 [quote from Jesus]: *"Again, truly I tell you that if two of you on earth agree about anything they ask for it, it will be done for them by my Father in heaven."*
Why does Jesus mention two people? Maybe so that one person could warn the other whenever the other person experienced selfish desires. We can't anything from God anyway, because what we *want* often isn't what we *need:* For example, when a person is filled with hatred God will not give them riches:
James 4,2: *"You do not have because you do not ask God. When you ask, you do not receive, because you ask with the wrong motives, that you may spend what you get on your pleasures."* Or:
1. John 3,17f: *"If anyone has material possessions and sees a brother or sister in need but has no pity on them, how can the love of God be in that person? Dear children, let us not love with words or speech but with actions and in truth. [...] Dear friends, if our hearts do not condemn us, we ... receive from him* [note: God] *anything we ask, because we* **keep his commands** *and do what pleases him."*
Ah, if we obey God's commandments, our prayers will be answered!
1. John 5,14f: *"This is the confidence we have in approaching God: that if we ask anything* **according to his will,** *he hears us."*

This means that God can only answer a prayer = grant a wish, if this corresponds to His will. **Does this mean that we can't have "wishes of our own"? No – because He has long placed** *our* **deepest,** *real* **(not selfish) desires in us, namely** *His* **will!** God can only bring His wishes = His will into the world or can only fulfil this wish = our prayer when we ask him with pure hearts, with which his will is also fulfilled. God wants us to ask Him instead of us trying to do it out of our own strength, resulting in exhaustion:
James 4,2: *"You covet but cannot get what you want, so you quarrel and fight. You do not have because you do not ask God."* In plain English:
Matthew 7,8 & Luke 11,10: *"For everyone who asks receives; the one who seeks finds; and to the one who knocks, the door will be opened."*

The most important thing is the right attitude of the heart. **This is because we only give God permission to help us in our lives through prayer! And God *wants* to help us!** Especially when we pray in the name of His Son, that is, when we explicitly say: "Father in heaven, God of Isaac, Abraham, and Jacob, in the name of Jesus I ask you for help with (this or that matter) ...". Folks these words are to be applied – and they work! **Dear readers: you can pray for yourself, for projects, ect., but also for other people** (the latter is called intercession). **God will hear you!**

Here is the scientific evidence that praying helps:
In 1988 Dr Randolph Byrd, a doctor from San Francisco, asked a group of local Christians to pray for 393 heart patients. Neither patients nor nurses knew that they were being prayed for. The result was clear: Patients suffered less heart failures, needed less medication and required fewer ventilation. Numerous follow-up studies came up with similar results. By the way: In these studies, however, only Christians prayed ... More information on this in the link below.[2]

Of course what happened next can almost be called a sabotage, here's why:
The famous atheist author **Richard Dawkins,** as one would expect, conducted counter studies in order to prove the inefficacy of prayer. He then compared prayer to a "lucky charm", which is sold to the sick by a trickster as a means of healing. But the following example is – sorry, Mr. Dawkins – quite weak, without substance: Dawkins describes in a very unobjective manner a "representative of God", who, with a Bible in his hand, prays for a cancer patient and then claims that God this patient to pay 10% of his salary (the "tithe") to the church: "How about a deductible donation today?"[3]
Here Dawkins mixes up two facts from the Bible in a way that shows that he had far too insufficiently concerned himself with the Bible!
Of course there a deceivers who twist and abuse God's word, but the following scriptures refute Mr. Dawkins:
1/2 A real Christian is never allowed to – and never will – ask for money in exchange for the word of God or prayers! Gott and His Son Jesus don't want that, period.

---

2   Bild der Wissenschaft online, Eberle, Ute, "Intercession with action at a distance", www.wissen- schaft.de/archiv/-/journal_content/56/12054/1595366/F%C3%BCrbitte-mit-Fernffekt/, March 1, 2003, accessed on December 6, 2017
3   Richard Dawkins Foundation online, "Prayers Are Just Superstition", de.richarddawkins.net/articles/gebete-sind-nur-aberglaube, August 25, 2014, demolished. on December 7, 2017

2/2 Tithing has **nothing** to do with healing prayer, tithing is the only challenge God gives us to "try" Him, to trust Him: Invest 10% of your net salary into the kingdom of God, meaning support those in need or Christian projects etc., and God return it you x-fold! While we are already taking about scientific studies: Have a look at chapter 6.3, step 6/7 – there you will read how a WithJesus-Staff conducted an empirical self-experiment and concluded that God indeed very generously reimburses tithing.

Mr. Dawkins this is a reprehensible allegation and gnaws at your credibility – sorry! You mix up two facts and suggest a generalizable message that Christians automatically request money for prayer from sick people. **Nonsense!** The fact is: **An incredible number of those seeking for help find consolation, hope and develop strength when they are prayed for – even when they know that they will die!** It is certainly difficult to create a study in this context, because how can it be covered by the study when a patient secretly prays, or someone prays for them? However, **the results are so significant** that even doctors publicly admit its efficacy. They not only have a job to lose, but also credibility. Here is a quote from **Dr. William Harris,** a doctor at the Saint Lukes Hospital in Kansas City: "This can hardly be explained without the existence of a kind of higher intelligence."[4]

To be fair: You can read something **very positive about Mr Dawkins** in chapter 2.5.
Conclusion of this chapter: Prayer helps, period.

NOT everything is predetermined!

One of the most precious gifts from God to us humans is **free will.** This is what distinguishes humans from animals. The famous author and aviator **Antoine de Saint-Exupéry** describes in his great adventure book **"Wind, sand and stars"** how his friend and comrade Henri Guillaumet, whose plane had crashed in the icy Andes and who was believed to be dead, made it back: He had laid himself in the snow several times, willing to die, but then he remembered that his wife would receive neither life insurance nor pension in the case his body was never to be found. So, he kept on crawling. Every step was a challenge, required will-

---

4   Bild der Wissenschaft online, Eberle, Ute, "Intercession with action at a distance", http: // www.wissen- schaft.de/archiv/-/journal_content/56/12054/1595366/F%C3%BCrbitte-mit-Fernffekt/, March 1, 2003, accessed on December 6, 2017

power. When after seven days (!!!) he was picked up on a street, he told his friend St. Exupéry: "I can tell you this: What I did, no animal could have done it!" We humans can decide whether we want to forgive someone or punch them in the face. We can decide whether we want to smoke a thousand cigarettes a day and then die miserably or take up the fight against this addiction and extend our lives (with Jesus' help it works!) – there would be enough work to do on this planet. What we hardly can imagine is that God already *knows beforehand* how we will decide! No wonder, God is independent from space and time – this is how he also could give us the prophecies in the Bible, see chapter 2.0. To designate the human destiny as "predetermined" is subjective and hypothetical, thus can't quite be correct. Even if someone wouldn't be able to give up their addiction, we could still pray together with them. **God will give us the strength to live a free and flourishing live – with our free will. And this makes us independent from predestination.**

2.5 Biblical Prophecies & Jesus – NOT Written "In Retrospect": Evidence

First of all, we want to refute the most common counterargument here: Was the Bible written "in retrospect"? This is very often asserted by non-believers or people from other faith groups in discussions with us, the WithJesus-Team. Our preferred way of responding to this argument is: "Ah, so after May 14th 1948!". Non-verbal reactions, such as puzzled faces, open mouths then ensue very often.

After that we like to tell them what God announced to mankind in the Old Testament through the prophets in a time span of 700 years, before Jesus was born

Isaiah 66,8: *"Who has ever heard of such things? Who has ever seen things like this? Can a country be born in a single day or a nation be brought forth in a moment?"* What does "a country born in a single day" mean? It means the following:

Contrary to all expectations and exactly after 1810 years of patient waiting by the Jews, the state of Israel was brought back to life *in a single day,* on May 14th 1948, after a democratic *majority* was surprisingly achieved at the UN.

Jesus' prophecy came true! One of the 6400 prophecies once again confirmed in the Bible!

Here is the full story to prove it: In the year 138 the Jews wanted to get rid of the Roman occupation in Israel in one last attempt, the Bar-Kochbar-uprising. Emperor Hadrian put down the uprising. Out of anger about the indomitable Jewish people, he wanted to delete the memory of Israel once and for all and ordered the renaming of Israel to "Palestine". Another disgrace lies behind this term: Palestine comes from "Pelishtim", which means "Philistines" – and these people were known to be among the worst enemies of the Jewish people.
Palestine was never a sovereign, recognized state with recognized borders.
Also, the West Bank were the Israeli provinces Judea and Samaria.
Thus: The "area" Palestine is the state of Israel.
Real Christians pray for a peaceful solution for both Muslims and Jews.

Over the course of the centuries, the Jews have been unfaithful to God again and again. They didn't give God the right to help them despite the fact that He had warned them several times. Therefore, He couldn't help them anymore – gruesome persecution and expulsion to all countries were the consequences, starting from 138 AD. **However, God had announced all of this – but also the future return of the Jews to their land Israel-through the prophets in the Old Testament long before Jesus.** Because of this, the Jews never gave up the hope to someday be able to return to Israel. (More info on pages 29 & 30 and in the book "Believing? Knowing!" by the WithJesus-Team)

The **"Madagascar Plan"** has existed since the 19th century: Madagascar was offered to the Jews in place of Israel – the Jews denied, because they trusted the biblical prophecy, which promised that they would get Israel back. During World War II, Ribbentrop, Heydrich and Eichmann, high ranking Nazi officers, reopened the Madagascar plan: The island was supposed to serve as "the final solution of the Jewish question", namely a ghetto and death island. After that, the island was a British mandate.
Hardly anyone was able to imagine or had hope of how and when the Land of Israel could ever arise again.

About 720 years before the birth of Jesus Christ, God gave the prophet Isaiah the prophecy for the re-emergence of Israel, which per the resolution of the UN, happened in only ONE day! The re-emergence of Israel was also announced in a 2200 year-old parchment scroll found in the caves Qumran[5] in 1947.

---

5 These "Dead Sea Scrolls" prove the authenticity of their biblical texts

Just ask older relatives who might have a Bible from *before* 1948 – even there the same prophecy of Isaiah, which came true on May 14th, 1948, is written: *"About a country, which came forth in only one day."* (Isaiah 66) With that the rumour that the Bible was written "in retrospect" is thus refuted.

We now refute another counterargument, often put forward: Didn't, theoretically then, every country come into being "in one day"? For example, through completion of a contract or something similar? Even if this was the case: Only Israel has this many prophecies and it was only for Israel so unexpected and unlikely for them to ever come true. **Counterargument refuted; prophecy confirmed.** But the Bible hold even more miracles in store: Since more than 3,500 years, the prophecies of the Bible are being fulfilled, with a success rate of 100% at that. They constitute concrete, precise announcements (no vague metaphors) about cities, people, countries, wars. Some of them we can even experience with our own eyes-today.

Attention, the following is important before you read the prophecies: Read how Jesus personally quotes the prophet Isaiah in the Bible for his listeners in **Matthew 13,14:** *"You will be ever hearing but never understanding; you will be ever seeing but never perceiving. For this people's heart has become calloused."* This means that non-Christians or people who don't have the Holy Spirit will read the words of Jesus and the Bible, yet they won't understand them.

Illustration 2: Not far from the Northwest bank of the Dead Sea are the Qumran caves, the place where the "Qumran Scrolls" were found. These caves are partially natural in origin but were also partially man-made by digging into the karst. They were even inhabited by people. Were they places of refuge for the Essenes? Were they writing workshops or synagogues? Opinions of archaeologists diverge.
But the scrolls found confirm that the content of the Bible is unchanged. ℗©**WITH JESUS**®

Therefore, *please* pray directly to God "in the name of Jesus to be filled with the Holy Spirit", so that He will open your heart and mind for the following biblical prophecies. The authors of these lines are aware that this might be a little strange for you, but simply do it, just as a child prays to God, in your own words.

Prophecies about cities:

The supernatural nature of the Bible is completely recognizable due to its precise information about cities, people, and countries. But it doesn't just predict happenings, but also *permanently valid* facts, e.g.:
*"This city will be destroyed **and** no longer or will be rebuilt!"*
This is a great risk for the prophets of the Bible, because:
They prophesied, for example, the destruction of a city **and** ...
... whether it should be rebuilt or not!
But where do cities come into being? Next to old, heavily frequented trade routes or shipping lanes. Therefore, it is very unusual for none of these cities to be rebuilt – something which would be sensible because building materials of the destroyed houses were there, and the old trade routes continued to be used. See the following example of **Nineveh** and **Babylon**.
The ruins of both cities were located at popular places or paths.
Yet these cities weren't rebuilt – prophecy confirmed.
The following happenings, announced up to 2700 years ago, demonstrably took place years after their prophecy and are valid until today:

Judgment of Nineveh
The destruction of Nineveh, located in what is now Iraq, was prophesied by the prophets Zephaniah and Nahum.
Zephaniah 2,14: *"He will make Nineveh a desolation, a dry waste like the desert. Herds shall lie down in her midst [...] even the owl and the hedgehog shall lodge in her capitals; devastation will be on the threshold; This is the exultant city that lived securely, that said in her heart »I am the one! And there is none else«. What a desolation she has become ..."*
Nahum 3,15: *"There the fire will consume you; the sword will cut you down."*
Bible: Zephaniah received this prophecy in 622 BC., at the time of the cultural reform of Joschija (647-609 BC.), king of the southern kingdom of Judah.
Historical fact: In August 612 BC Nineveh was destroyed by the Medes and Babylonians. Prophecy confirmed.

Fall of Sinful Babylon

Isaiah 13,21: *"Babylon, the jewel of kingdoms, the pride and glory of the Babylonians, **will be overthrown** by God like Sodom and Gomorrah. She will never be inhabited or lived in through all generations; there no nomads will pitch their tents, there no shepherds will rest their flocks. But desert creatures will lie there, jackals will fill their houses; there the owl will dwell, and the wild goats will leap about. Hyenas will inhabit her strongholds, jackals her luxurious palaces."*

Bible: Isaiah was active between 740-701 BC.

Historical fact: In the following century, Babylon was afterwards destroyed twice (including 689 BC by Sennacherib). After it was revived for a short time by Alexander the Great, the Roman emperor Trajan only saw ruins in 115 BC. It is said that in the late antiquity asphalt was extracted from there. What a decline of what was once perhaps the greatest city in the world with up to 200,000 inhabitants. In the Bible its destruction had been announced many years beforehand. Prophecy confirmed.

Sidon got a second chance and is still inhabited today.

Ezekiel 28,22: *"... and say: 'This is what the Sovereign Lord says: "I am against you, Sidon, and among you I will display my glory. You will know I am the Lord, when I inflict punishment on you ..."*

Through Ezekiel God announces His judgment over Sidon, but not its eternal destruction: Located between Beirut and Tire, this "fishing town", the literal meaning of Sidon, is still inhabited. Prophecy confirmed.

Samaria on the other hand, is deserted to this day:

Micha 1,6-7: *"Therefore I will make **Samaria a heap of rubble**, a place for planting vineyards. I will pour her stones into the valley and lay bare her foundations. All her idols will be broken into pieces; all her temple gifts will be burned with fire; I will destroy all her images."*

The prophet Micah was active at around 740-700 BC. Samaria, which was practising idolatry (possibly with child sacrifices!), was destroyed 722 BC by the Assyrians and 107 BC by the Hasmoneans. Prophecy confirmed.

Chorazin, Betsaida, Capernaum – only ruins are left there;

Matthew 11,20: *"Woe to you, Chorazin! Woe to you, Bethsaida! ... And you, Capernaum [...] No, you will go down to Hades!"* These are the final words Jesus said personally! And now have a guess – right, all that is left of these three cities are ruins. For example, Capernaum was destroyed by an earthquake in 746 BC. But there was another city, a fourth one at the Sea of Galilee, Tiberias. This one was not mentioned by Jesus and still is inhabited by 40,000 people and flourishing – it is the biggest city in the Jordan Valley. **Prophecies confirmed – the Bible has thousands more of them in store for us!**

Prophecies About Israel - An Excerpt

There are many prophecies about Israel and especially Jerusalem, here is one of them: In front of his disciples Jesus prophesied an astonishing detail about the temple in Jerusalem after its destruction by the Romans in
Matthew 24,2: *"Truly I tell you, not one stone here will be left on another; every one will be thrown down."*
40 years later, the Roman occupiers burned down the temple. After that every stone of the temple was actually turned over again, because the Romans were looking for part of the molten golden domed roof – prophecy fulfilled!
But there also is a multitude of great, positive prophecies for Israel and its capital Jerusalem – more on the following pages in chapter 6.3 and in the "Believing? Knowing!" by the WithJesus-Team.

Even less heeded prophecies in the Bible, however, are coming true now, right now: Since around 2016 there are fish in the Dead Sea! For millennia this had been impossible and unthinkable due to the high salt content in the Dead Sea- but not for one prophet in the Old Testament, namely
Ezekiel 47,8f: *"He [note: God] said … "This water flows toward the … Dead Sea. [...] There will be large numbers of fish, because this water flows there and makes the salt water fresh; so where the river flows everything will live."* [6]

Future events about Israel and the Jews were already announced in the 3,500-year-old prophecies of Moses – *all* of them came true! Likewise, the same was done through the prophets of the Old Testament and the last one of them lived 450 years before Christ.
All events happened and they still do until our time!
Here are the facts – they are inexplicable for us humans because everything came true: Moses gives blessings to the Jewish people if they obey God. But they were unfaithful to God and "locked" Him out of their lives, worshipped

---

6 livenet.ch online, Gerber, Daniel, "Prophecy comes true – first fish in the Dead Sea sighted", http://www.livenet.ch/news/gesellschaft/wissen/staunen/296222-erste_fische_im_toten_meer_gesicht.html? utm_source = dlvr.it & utm_medium = facebook, August 11, 2016, sold. at the 7.2.2018

idols made from wood or stone and much more. Therefore, God announced the consequences to his people via Moses in
Deuteronomy 28: 32-34, 37, 64-65: *"Your sons and daughters will be given to another nation, and you will wear out your eyes watching them day after day, powerless to lift a hand. A people that you do not know will eat what your land and labor produce, and you will have nothing but cruel oppression all your days. The sights you see will drive you mad.*
You will become a thing of horror, a byword and object of ridicule among all the peoples where the Lord will drive you. **And the Lord will scatter you among all nations, from one end of the earth to the other.**
Among those nations you will find no repose, no resting place for the sole of your foot. There the Lord will give you an anxious mind, eyes weary with longing, and a despairing heart."

What a risk to the credibility of prophets in the Bible it must have been to announce the *complete dispersion* to a people – and yet it came true.
Which appalling announcements of persecution, murder and misery were made – and yet everything happened up until the Holocaust.
God warned the Jews, invited them to trust Him, to not become unfaithful. Yet, the Jewish people left God, became unfaithful to Him, locked Him out of their lives.
God respects people's free will, which is why He couldn't help the Jews anymore. Although he wanted!
We Christians, living in the New Covenant and willing to live out the New Testament and the love and mercy of Jesus, need great willpower to read about these atrocities.

Yet God gives the expelled Jews already as early as 1500 BC (!) – the return from all over the world back to their homeland Israel in:
Deuteronomy 30, 1-5: *"When all these blessings and curses I have set before you come on you and you take them to heart wherever the Lord your God disperses you among the nations, and when you ... obey him with all your heart and with all your soul ... then the Lord your God will ... gather you again from all the nations where he scattered you.*
He will bring you to the land that belonged your ancestors."

This country means nothing else than: Israel.

Prophecies About Israel - 3 Points to Confirm

1/3 In the prophecy of Moses (Deut. 30, 1-5) mentioned belowon the lefthand side the Jewish people are addressed in a situation of displacement all over the world, unthinkable at the time of this statement, because it was about 1500 years *before* the dispersion!

2/3 The return to a country, namely Israel, is announced to the Jews even though they haven't been driven out of it yet and even though this country did not exist at all from 138 AD to May 14, 1948 (In 138 AD Emperor Hadrian forced a mock name upon Israel from which the term "Palestine" ultimately originated, see page 25). Within the span of these 1810 years nobody could imagine that Israel would ever exist again or that the Jews would ever be able to return there (the "Madagascar Plan", see page 25).
Nevertheless: Israel emerged anew. Prophecy confirmed.

Beware, a risk of dilution: Some liberal theologians, esotericists, atheists and critics interpret this return of the Jews to apply for the time after the Babylonian exile in 539 BC. **Wrong.**
Prophet Amos proves that this interpretation is incorrect and delivers a confirmation of the supernatural nature of this Bible prophecy:
Amos 9,14: *"I will plant Israel in their own land, **never again to be uprooted from the land I have given them,"** says the Lord your God!"*
The emphasis is on: *" ... plant ... never again to be uprooted!"*
Proof:
After the return from Babylonia in 539 BC the Jews were "torn out"= expelled by the Romans from 138 AD onwards. Therefore, the return of the Jews can only mean the time of AFTER the Romans, especially the waves of immigration at the end of the 19th century caused by persecution (France, Russia), **especially from Germany from 1933!**

Isaiah 66,8: *"Who has ever heard of such things? Who has ever seen things like this? Cab a country be born in a day or a nation be brought forth **in a single day?**"*
On May 14th 1948 the State of Israel was brought again to life *"**in a single day**"* through a democratic UNO resolution on November 29th, 1947. The centuries-old hope of the Jewish people came into being, in spite of most of the world's expectations. Ever since that day more and more Jews have poured in to their old homeland. What a unique event in human history!

Critics object to that and say: "Wasn't every country created 'in one day'?" This is easy to refute, due to the fact that no war preceded the happenings in Israel in 1948 and also due to the fact that David Ben Gurion called Israel back to life *in one day*. Besides, how many countries have such prophecies like Israel does? None.[7]

3/3 Jews from all over the world are relentlessly moving back to Israel, since 1948 and also NOW – according to the Bible, they will never again be driven out again. Here are more prophecies, the fulfilment of which we can witness right now. We only have to open newspapers or listen to the news. Ezekiel and Jeremiah lived about 600 years before Jesus:

Ezekiel 34,13: *"I will bring them out from the nations and gather them from the countries, and **I will bring them into their own land**. I will pasture them on the mountains of Israel, in the ravines and in all the settlements in the land."*

Jeremiah 31,8: *"See, I will bring them **from the land of the north** and gather them from the ends of the earth. Among them will be the blind and the lame, expectant mothers and women in labor; **a great throng will return.**"*

What is "the land of the north"? Quite straightforward: Russia is located in the northern Israel, especially Ukraine, from where terribly discriminated and persecuted Jews – more than a million – especially fled to Israel in the 1930s and during the era of Stalin. **Prophecy fulfilled.**

In summary, it can be said that
• the expulsion of the Jews
• the decline and resurrection of Israel
• the return of Jews living scattered around the world
were predicted down to the last detail and continue to happen to the present day. Biblical prophecies began in the time of Moses (about 3500 years ago).

The precision of prophecies in the Bible can only be deemed "supernatural" by logically thinking people. King Frederick the Great (1712-1786) once asked his **General Hans Joachim von Zieten** whether he could given him proof of the existence of God. Zieten said: "Your Majesty – the Jews". Von Zieten recognized the miracle of the prophecies that God shows us with the story of the Jews in the Bible.

---

7 We from the WithJesus-Team also wish that Muslims can live in peace in Israel. But the subject is a complex one and there are people who want to constantly stir up war here – no, not the Jews. More one this can be found in the book "Believing? Knowing!" by the WithJesus-Team

Prophecies about Jesus: Historio-Archaeological Evidence that He lived

If you have only started reading this book at this part here: In the Bible there are around 3000 prophecies that have come true. 300 of them are about Jesus' life and work, including the smallest details, from His birth and also about His life and work beyond our present times. And from the time of David, a thousand years before the birth of Christ, at that! And all of them have come true, with lots of evidence ... neither comprehensible nor explainable for our limited human logic ...

Even though the Romans came over Jerusalem and its surroundings in 70 AD, setting fire to the second temple, demolishing buildings and killing countless residents, **many concrete proofs of the existence of Jesus exist:**

This is what the Roman historian **Tacitus,** who is considered reliable, tells us in the year 116: "In order to get rid of the rumours, he [note: Emperor Nero] put the blame on others and imposed the most exquisite punishments on those hated for their crimes, called 'Chrestians' by the people. The author of this name is Christ who had been executed under the rule of Tiberius under the procurator Pontius Pilate."

Gaius Suetonius Tranquillus, better known by the name **Sueton** was a Roman writer, biographer from Caesar to Domitian, but also the main secretary of **Emperor Hadrian.** Under the rule of the latter he wrote the following in his imperial biographies De vita Caesarum in 129 AD, Chapter 25,4: "He [note: Emperor Claudius] drove the Jews, who were incited by a certain Christos and continually caused unrest, out from Rome."

The historian **Thallus** wrote a three-volume historiography of the Eastern Mediterranean, which does not exist anymore, but whose content was cited by several other authors: In 221 AD the Christian chronicler Sextus Julius Africanus wrote about the Judgemental eclipse, which the non-believing Thallus wanted to dismiss as solar eclipse: "Thallus calls this eclipse a solar eclipse in the third book of the histories. It seems to me that this is against reasonable insight." Because Sextus testifies that Jesus was crucified before or during the feast of the Passover, which only takes places during a full moon. **Solar eclipses normally take place during a new moon – thus, this darkness could only have been a supernatural one.**

33

The well-known Jewish Roman historian **Flavius Josephus** (actually Joseph ben Mathitjahu, about 37 AD- 100 AD in Rome) reports **astonishing things.** In his "Antiquitates judaicae 18.3" he calls James the "brother of Jesus, called Christ." Here is the original text of Flavius: "Around this time there lived a Jesus, a wise man, if he can rightly be called a man. For he did amazing deeds ... He was the Christ ... who appeared to them alive on the third day, just as the prophets had prophesied these and ten thousand other things about him." **Wow!**

Or, in another reading: "At that time there lived a wise man called Jesus. His conduct was good, and he was known to be virtuous. And many of the Jews and of other nations became his disciples. Pilate sentenced him to crucifixion and to death. But those who became his disciples did not leave his fellowship. They reported that he appeared to them three days after his crucifixion and that he was alive; so maybe he was the Messiah, whose miracles the prophets reported." [8]

Hey – a Jewish historian contemplates that Jesus might be the Messiah – hardly believable, since Jesus was actually a "competitor" of Judaism. Even more astonishing: In 67 AD Flavius fought against the Romans, survived and in his captivity prophesied that Vespasian and his son Titus would become emperors – when this actually happened two years later, he was allowed to work as a freelance interpreter and become an intermediary, received Roman citizenship, a hefty pension with a villa (!) and was able to continue writing. **In the Bible, God promises new talents to people who follow Him or Jesus- and blessings to those who bless His people, the Jews, (Genesis 12:3). God probably blessed Flavius in the form of a prophetic talent and a pension, because thanks to his mediation, captured Jews were released.**

A wonderful story: Simon Petrus' house, a simple residential building, is located in Capernaum. **131 chalk inscriptions found on the walls of the time of Jesus tell of the presence of Peter and of Jesus!** It is the house in which Jesus healed Peter's mother-in-law, as described in

Matthew 8,14: "*When Jesus came into Peter's house, he saw Peter's mother-in-law lying in bed with a fever. He touched her hand and the fever left her, and she got up and began to wait on him.*"

The house still exists, Capernaum is in the north of the lake Galilee and you

---

8 Vom "Testimonium Flavianum" – gibt es zahlreiche Quellen, u.a. hier: impantokratoros. gr online, "Nichtchristliche Zeugnisse des 1. und 2. Jahrhunderts über Christus", https://www. impantokratoros.gr/zeugnisse-Christus.de.aspx, abger. am 9.5.2018

can visit comfortably: Above the archaeological site, the **Church of St. Peter** was built on stilts. This was done so that on the one hand, the remains of Peter's house and of the excavation work could be protected from the weather, and on the other, that the visitors could admire a real whereabout of Jesus through a big window in the floor – a brilliant idea.

Jesus, the Son of God – Supernatural Evidence That He Is Still Alive

Some time ago the author of these lines had a conversation with a professor at a German university, who did research on and taught subjects, which came close to supernatural phenomena. He put the "question of questions" about Jesus in a nutshell: **"Jesus existed, that is historically secured. But the questions is-was He really the Son of God?"**
Based on the facts provided here, we are convinced: Yes. And he's still alive? Yes, all indications are for it. Because if you dive deeper into the matter and think about it systematically, you only reach this insight.
For the prophecies in the Bible all came true with a quota of 100%, and they still apply.
These supernatural announcements in the Bible are unique within the religions of the world – there is hardly anything on earth we can trust more than them. No, they were not written afterwards. This is proven in the preceding chapters of this book.
And in chapter 2.6 you may have probably already read the thoughts of leading Quantum physicists – they *physically* confirm the possibility of eternal life, multidimensionality, and talk more and more about God ... Yes, right, scientists, globally respected physicists are saying something like that.
There are more than 300 supernatural prophecies in the Bible about Jesus, which specifically only predict Jesus and happenings of His life. Some of them originate from a time *over a thousand years BEFORE Jesus' life.* Of course, you can only find a fraction of these announcements in this very book, due to limited space. The rest can be found in the Bible. Here is an excerpt of prophecies from the **Old Testament (=OT)** and their confirmations in the **New Testament (=NT)**:

OT Exodus 12,46 (approx. 1300 BC): *"Do not break any of the bones."* [note: Jesus]. Here Moses preempts a situation of the Saviour's crucifixion. More on the next page ...

OT Psalm 34,21 (approx. 1000 BC): *"He keeps all his bones, **not one of them will be broken.**"*

OT Zechariah 12,10 (approx. 520 BC.): *"... They will look on me, the one they have **pierced,** and they will mourn for him as one mourns for an only child ... for a firstborn son."*

NT John 19,34 (at the time of Jesus): *"The soldiers therefore came and broke the legs of the first man who had been crucified with Jesus, and then those of the other. But when they came to Jesus and found that he was already dead, they **did not break his legs.** Instead, one of the soldiers **pierced Jesus' side with a spear** ..."*

Explanation: Since no dead person was allowed to hang on the cross on the Sabbath, the soldiers broke the legs of the sufferers hanging on the cross, so that they would die faster. This way they could not lift themselves up with their nailed legs, lost strength, could not pull themselves up with their arms, their lungs, expanded from hanging could no longer use up stale air and so they, who were condemned to death, suffocated more quickly. As inhumane this may sound, the crucified people actually saw this as a move of grace, because it shortened the unbearable pain. This info only refers to the inconceivable, unimaginable sacrifice that Jesus suffered for us – His bones were not broken.

OT Psalm 22,17 (approx. 1000 BC.): *"Dogs surround me, a pack of villains encircles me; they pierce my hands and my feet."*

NT John 19,17 (at the time of Jesus): *"Carrying his own cross, he went out to the place of the Skull (which in Aramaic is called Golgotha). There they crucified him."*

Explanation: When David wrote the Psalm above around 1000 BC, the practice of crucifixion existed only among Phoenicians and Assyrians, but not among the Jews. And often the condemned had "only" handcuffed hands and feet, so as to lengthen their agony. But David "saw" prophetically that Jesus would be "pierced" – extraordinary out of his perspective, since at that time only other nations "pierced" peoples at crucifixion. And yet it happened that way.

OT Psalm 22,19 (approx. 1000 BC.): *"They **divide my clothes among** them and cast lots for my garment."*

NT John 19,23 (at the time of Jesus): *"When the soldiers crucified Jesus, they took his clothes, dividing them into four **shares,** one for each of them, with the undergarment remaining. This garment was seamless, woven in one piece from top to bottom. 'Let's not tear it,' they said to one another. 'Let's decide by **lot** who will get it!'"*

David "saw" in another prophecy that the soldiers would decide by lot who would get Jesus' clothes – even this detail is listed as a point of confirmation of the supernatural origin of this content. *You cannot arrange something like that!*

OT Isaiah 40,3 (approx. 720 BC): *"A voice of one calling: 'In the wilderness prepare the way for the Lord; make straight in the desert a highway for our God!'"*
NT Matthew 3,1-2 (at the time of Jesus): *"In those days John the Baptist came, preaching in the wilderness of Judea and saying, 'Repent for the kingdom of heaven has come near!'"*
Explanation: The prophet Isaiah "hears" – approx. 720 years before Jesus' birth – how John the Baptist is calling out Jesus.

OT Isaiah 9,6 (approx. 720 BC): *"For to us a child is born, to us **a son is given,** and the government will be on his shoulders. And he will be called Wonderful Counsellor, Mighty God, Everlasting Father, Prince of Peace."*
NT Matthew 16,16, Jesus asks the apostles: *"'Who do you say I am?'* Simon Peter answered *'You are the Messiah, the Son of the living God.'"*

OT Daniel Chapter 9, Verses 25 & 26 (approx. 600 BC.): *"From the time the word goes out to **restore and rebuild Jerusalem** until the Anointed One, the ruler [note: Jesus], comes, there will be **'sevens' [note: 1 week]** and **sixty-two 'sevens'.** It will be rebuilt with streets and a trench, but in times of trouble. After the sixty-two 'sevens', the Anointed One will be put to death and will have nothing."*
But he can see even further: By "week" Daniel signifies the "year week", namely seven years. We can calculate it precisely: 7x7= **49 years, 62** year weeks x 7= **434 years.**
49 + 434 = 483 years, 483 years after 445 BC. = 38 AD Combining these numbers with the changes of the Gregorian calendar, Daniel's calculation directly leads us to the year 32 AD, which is the year of Jesus' death, the *Anointed One to be put to death!* **Prophecy confirmed.**

In case somebody voices disagreement, shouting that this prophetic calculation of Daniel could have also been written "afterwards": it was already mentioned in the first translation of the Bible into Greek, the so-called **Septuagint.** This term denotes the number of 72 scholars, who translated the Bible independently from each other, in order to arrive at a final error-free product – thus, their work could also be compared like this. The Septuagint, however, was completed between 250 and 100 *before* Christ, while the translation of the book of Daniel was finished at around 164 BC. Both confirm the supernatural origin of Daniel's prophecy.

Critics also believe that Jesus made an entrance riding on a donkey on Palm Sunday and by doing so, also fulfilled a prophecy "in retrospect", see **Zechariah 9,9:** *"Rejoice greatly, Daughter Zion! Shout, Daughter Jerusalem! See, your king comes to you, righteous and victorious, lowly and riding on a donkey, on a colt, the foal of a donkey"* [9]

What – are you saying that Jesus supposedly re-enacted this "in retrospect" so that he could use it and later on refer to it? Nonsense! **The truth:** Imagine how many people He would have had to place around the surroundings, the streets, instructing them to wave palm fronds and lay clothes beneath his feet, just like a director. Besides that, our source also claims that this incident was not found in other documents apart from the Bible and that it was "not confirmed in any other part of the New Testament". Incorrect. Here is the ...

... **Refutation:** It is written in Matthew 21, Mark 11, Luke 19 and John 12 that Jesus entered Jerusalem riding on a donkey. To now call this incident a falsehood just because it cannot be found in *any other text* is very strange to Christians. Furthermore, a reply to this cannot be found anywhere.

Additionally: How else would the prophecy come true other than Jesus *just* entering on a donkey? And the numerous prophecies about His death on the cross, including all their details? How many extras would there have been needed in order to deceivingly act out a very complex, almost infeasible to direct sequence of actions of a crowd, which was barely controllable? And if all of this was a lie, would Jesus then, in order to "artificially" fulfil a prophecy, have needed to die on the cross in a horrendous manner? Then what for?

Dear readers if you think logically: Even though this event could have failed because of millions of things *it happened after all.* And just as it was prophesied in the Bible, Christianity is growing, Israel was reestablished and many more. Jesus is the Son of God and through all these prophecies, which He "dictated to the prophets for our edification and salvation" God has glorified Himself in Him. Thank you.

Bible prophecies = verifiable supernaturalness: The prophets could not know these specifics on their own. Something dead could also not tell them, only the living God, who, independent from our structures of space and time, announces secrets to us, because He loves us.

---

9 heise.de online, Telepolis, Schmeh, Klaus, "Prove that the prophecies that have arrived Bible is the word of God?", www.heise.de/tp/features/Beweisen-eingetroffene-Prophezeiungen-that-the-Bible-is-God's-Word-3407938.html, Sept. 17, 2006, aborted. on March 28, 2018

This only happens in the Bible.

Even details of Jesus' life and execution are announced in advance and come true precisely: That He will be pierced, but that His bones would not be broken. That His clothes would be divided, but also that He is the God of God and the Saviour, who would be announced through John in the wilderness.

One of the most beautiful reassurances is announced by Jesus personally, in **Matthew 18,20:** *"For where two or three gather in my name, there am I with them."*
Jesus says this with any time constraints, so it still applies today. This means ...

... even when you only talk with friends about Jesus today, Jesus will be in your midst with the God's Holy Spirit.

And that is confirmed aptly in
Hebrews, 13,8: *"Jesus Christ is the same yesterday and today and forever!"*

Conclusion of this chapter — incredible:

The Bible predicts events, which also apply for the present, with incredible precision. About cities, people, countries and happenings.

These predictions *can be shown* to come from the time *before* these events.

All predictions have been fulfilled and *are still valid today.*
Even those that no one thought possible – see Israel.

Us humans can neither with our brains, nor with our consciousness, our intelligence, our senses, our mind comprehend, how something like this can work.

Despite conducting the most intensive research, we, the WithJesus-Team, have found precise prophecies, that came true,
exclusively in the Bible and in prophetic books by Christian authors.
(The well-known "prophecies of the Nostradamaus" are too metaphorical and therefore cannot be counted) What do we infer from these inconsistent facts?
Please turn the page ...

We can therefore only come to one single conclusion:
1/4   The Bible was *inspired supernaturally,* that is, "dictated" by God.
2/4   That's why you can trust the Bible without reservation – the content emphasizes this because it proves consistent facts.
3/4   The one, true, only God proves himself exclusively through the Bible.
4/4   The Bible proves to us, for the edification of all people: *God is alive!*

More on archaeological and historical evidence of biblical content can be found in the book "Believing? Knowing!" of the WithJesus-Team.

2.6 Further logical, physical evidence – there MUST be "more"!

In November 2019, a WithJesus-Staff wanted to travel to a WithJesus video shoot. The trip was intended to be combined with a small family vacation, but unfortunately money was very tight. So, he prayed with his with on Sunday evening: "God, if you want us to shoot this video, then please, as a means of confirmation, send somebody, who doesn't know anything about the whole situation and donates 500€ to us – until 5pm on Tuesday, please". His wife still was unsure if this was alright for God, but ... isn't God almighty? Didn't God create an incredibly large universe full of abundance? When the WithJesus-Staff returned home at 2:30 pm on Tuesday, he saw that the car of a friend of his wife was parked in front of their door. This friend of hers had "had the impression to give the family 500€", yet she had repeatedly pushed it back all the way into November: "But then I thought, I have to do it now!"
The WithJesus-Team is very grateful to this humble woman!

At around 4am in the spring of 1988 one of our WithJesus-Staff drove home with a car he had borrowed from his friends. He drove home very tired, the same as usual. It was freezing cold; he was the only driver on the highway and already saw the lights of his hometown flickering in the black winter night sky. At that time, he was 22 years old and in the midst of his Sturm und Drang-period, before he became a Christian. He was convinced that he had his occasional microsleep under control. Not even close. After about 55 of 70 km (note: 34 of 43 miles) he suddenly heard a loud call: his first name was called as if somebody would call him from two meters away! He opened his eyes in shock and in that moment saw how the guardrails on the left were approaching him.

Right behind that a massive concrete bridge pillar was coming, so he veered the car sharply across the full width of the highway, so that he could get the car under control again on the wet, snowy road, at the last moment.
Right, he had fallen asleep! His heart racing, he slowly continued his ride home, arriving there wide-awake because of the adrenaline.
He would never do that again, he resolved firmly.

Back then, he already considered many of the crazy dares, which his friends considered cool, as a mockery of the sanctity of life.
But this situation was beyond reason.
Most likely he owed his life to this call.
Only – who had called him? His subconscious? The universe? A Guardian Angel?
Or maybe ... God?

We Christians could cite a thousand such examples.
There has to be more than we see and usually believe.

Further Logical Evidence for God

In ancient Greece and in the Middle Ages, people believed in the so-called **Spontaneous Generation** – first of all, this theory is nonsense: it was believed that stuffing containers with old rags and garbage would "create" mice. Or that putting rotten food, rotten fruit or rotten meat into a container would "by itself" create vermin. Mice were said to be created out of sweat – see illustration 3 on the next page.

After all, we have arrived at the glorious realization that every living being (even atheists :-)) need a "creator" in order to live, i.e. some kind of mother and father. But, in turn, who has created them? And if we retrace this scenario a little, who is the "creator" of this process? Is it really just... "nature"?
Let us examine the basic law "As on a small scale, so on a large scale" on the level of the entire universe – on that of the phenomenon of *life:*￼

a **nature,** *a* **universe that brings forth living, individual, communicative, social (more or less, clear the throat), intelligent and creative beings** (hey, that means us, humans!), **must have at least the aspect of life, intelligence, communication ability and creativity *within itself!*** Because how should a

41

dead universe "create" living beings? Can, for example, a stone become a bird? Life cannot arise from something dead. That would be metaphysically impossible. And ridiculously illogical too.

Shouldn't the principle of life then flood through the whole universe? Shouldn't the principle of hearing, seeing, thinking, the principle of individuality then be present everywhere in the universe – in the form of a living God? **The Bible once again sums that up in a brilliantly in Psalm 94,9:** *"Does he who fashioned the ear not hear? Does he who formed the eye not see?"*

Further Physical Evidence for God

First a quote from **Albert Einstein:** "It is absolutely possible that unexpected worlds are hidden beyond the perception of our senses!"

Illustration 3:
This is how one imagined the so-called "Spontaneous Generation" in ancient Greece up until the Middle Ages: Food scraps and old rags were stuffed into a barrel so that life should soon arise "by itself". ℗©**WITH JESUS**®

Meanwhile the glorious realization has been made that every living being needs some kind of mother and/or father species. This is also how the Bible describes God: As the father of us all, who fills out the entire universe – please read Psalm 94,6 above

God, Bible, heaven, angels – all fairy tales or physically justifiable reality?
One can "physically prove" a human: They can be touched, have their temperature taken, protein and amino acids are present in their body, electric impulses in their nerves make their muscles twitch.
The prophecies in the Bible confirm that we are dealing with the one, living God here (chapter 2.2).

If we don't want to believe in fairy tales or fantasies, then we should also be capable of physically proving the existence of God and paradise, right?

If several God were to exist, which God would then have created the others? Since there is *one* principle that is the same everywhere in the universe, we can assume that there is only *one* God. Every human is born the same, everyone has to die. The same laws prevail everywhere, f.ex.: gravity, the theory of relativity, the reaction of chemical elements – even 25 galaxies away from us.

The esoteric sounding phrase "As on a small scale, so on a large scale" is, among others, named **"basic morphological patterns"** in real science – these patterns exist everywhere. A good example is the atomic model by the physicist Niels Bohr. Doesn't it look very similar to a small solar system? The electrons are circling around the nuclei made up of protons and neutrons – just like planets around the sun, see the illustration below.

Or the phenomenon of spiral shapes: these can be found anywhere in nature: in galaxies, or in snails and in the form of any DNA, the so-called double helix. Take a look at the lather in your Bathtub when it gushes down the drain – it

Illustration 4: *This is the model of an atom by Niels Bor (1885-1962), the famous Danish physicist. Evenh if an atom has a more complex structure in reality – in principle it works similar to a solar system:*
As on a small scale, so on a large scale.

℗©**WITH JESUS**®

too often takes the form of one spiral nebulae of a galaxy, often even with the characteristic arms! Each bubble is a star. Just a liiiiiittle bit smaller, because light takes about 100.000 years to cross our galaxy, the Milky Way.

There are rocks that, when cut through, display internal structures that look like a photo of the American prairie: different layers of sand including the table mountains known from the Wild West movies – that is also called basic morphological pattern. Many scientists worldwide are investigating, how "as on a small scale, so on a large scale" is possible.

So, it is, according to the laws of physics and the principles of this universe, not possible that "something comes out of nothing". Especially not something alive that is aware of its "I" and is creative etc. The **first thermodynamic principle** tells us that: "The energy of a closed system remains unchanged. Accordingly, various forms of energy can transform themselves into each other, but *energy can neither be created out of nothing nor can it be destroyed."*

Let us continue to spin this thought a little further: **That would mean that the principle of life itself must have existed before us** – something, which in turn, the Bible could confirm that God has always been there.

That would mean that "life" exists independently of our body. That would also mean that our "box of flesh"*, our body (*quote from a brilliant pastor :-)) can fall apart, but our soul could continue to exist. **Life after death, as promised by the Bible, can't be a fairytale land, but instead should – however, even if not yet – be physically explainable.**

Even the second thermodynamic principle fails because of the miracle of creation: "In a system that is left to itself order doesn't grow, but disorder!" The scientific term for this disorder is "entropy", for example the chaos of environmental pollution on our planet: first the ore in the mountains, the oil under the earth. Then plastic ends up in the ocean and junk cars dripping with old oil end up in the garbage dumps of this planet or in the forest.

Thus, theoretically there should be total chaos after the biggest explosion of all time, the **Big Bang. But no physicist in the world can explain, why a universe full of fascinating order, which also makes life possible, has emerged from this!** From where does the WithJesus-Team know this fact? Personally from a physicist! (also see chapter Near death experiences).

Why does one of the brightest minds of mankind, the locally known physicstinkerer **Albert Einstein** say: "The old man [note: he meant God] doesn't roll the dice?"

Why did the highly intelligent, but not even devout astronaut **Eugene Cernan** realize as he stood on the moon with Apollo 17 in December 1972, looking into space that "None of this can be a coincidence!"[10]

Why is the renowned Astrophysicist **Dr. Harald Lesch** from the University of Munich a Christian, testifying his belief in God on television in front of an audience of millions?[11]

Why did the matter of the universe extend exactly to the right extent after the Big Bang? A bit slower and everything would have collapsed, a bit faster and it couldn't have "clumped" together in places (so-called density fluctuations), out of which the celestial bodies emerged.

Also, nobody knows the reason behind the Big Bang in the midst of the previous inconceivable density of all matter, called "singularity". This denotes a state in which the entire universe "squeezed" itself into one point, beyond space or time. The previously mentioned physicist Dr. Harald Lesch for this reason "the unmoved first mover".
Or was it God who wanted to turn on the light?
Genesis 1,3: *"And God said, 'Let there be light' and there was light."*

And ... why does *anything at all* exist? Why is there actually not nothing? It would be much more logical if there was nothing at all! For example, please imagine a completely empty universe and in it a single stone the size of a fist. And suppose we could look at the whole thing "from the outside" (Yes, that is illogical, and it is only an assumption – please no letters to the editor). Wouldn't this stone be an unexplainable miracle? How much more *is life* on our planet, our inventiveness, our curiosity, the great intellectual, artistic or medical achievements a miracle? This planet could be so beautiful!

In the primordial soup experiment by Stanley Millers and Harold C. Urey (see illustration on following page) a sealed container was filled with an assumed, hypothetical primordial atmosphere: water, methane, ammonia, hydrogen and carbon monoxide.
Then little bolts of lightning were sent inside. This is how, according to the researchers, biomolecules, and simple elements of amino acids, the first buil-

10 Statement by E. Cernan in the BBC documentary "In The Shadow Of The Moon", 2007
11 Prof. Dr. Harald Lesch in Johannes B. Kerner's talk show on March 4th, 2009 on ZDF

45

ding blocks of life were created "out of nothing". But apart from the fact that most of them disintegrated and that one still cannot demonstrate how they can combine each other to form larger structures:

Stop, Mr. Miller and Mr. Urey – if you wanted to prove with your experiment that the theory of evolution and the creation of life are possible without God, then the content of your test tube is not a complete view of things – we need to look at the experiment *completely!* This also includes the big test tube with the primordial soup, the installations to initiate the electrical lightning *and the intelligence(s),* who were standing behind it – namely Mr. Miller and Mr. Urey *themselves.* They manufactured and put together all the pipelines and vessels, filled them with gas, started the power lines and pressed the button for the lightning bolts!

With all trials and experiments where researchers try to generate living matter out of inanimate matter, it is like this: Without a researcher there is no experi-

Illustration 5: The *"primordial soup experiment"* by Mr. Miller and Mr. Urey. Yeah, the two of them and their co-workers may have looked a little different, but one can roughly imagine the whole thing like this. ℗©**WITH JESUS**®

ment – **There is only a result with a creator who pushes the power button for the experiment.** As on a small scale, so on a large scale.

But it gets even more incredible: **Leading quantum physicists worldwide are increasingly speaking more often about God and find Him in the results of their experiments.** For example, Professor **Antoine Suarez** from the University of Geneva: "A powerful, invisible intelligence is at work here: God, angels or whatever!"[12]

Erwin Schrödinger, Austrian mathematician, quantum physicist and Nobel laureate, also believes in his work "My World View" that we "are a single whole, one consciousness!" Where do these thoughts of physicists that are surprising to us come from? Here is a small introduction to their world:

As early as 1802, the doctor Thomas Young discovered the famous **Double Slit Experiment** (see Ill. 6 and 7 on the next pages):
Light is projected onto a disk in which there are two slits. Theoretically two light spots should be visible on the projection surface behind it – but there are several! This shows that light quanta behave like waves. Like when you drop two stones into a pond: the circular expanding waves layer themselves in an interference pattern, i.e., they partially extinguish each other, partially intensify each other, enabling multiple spots of light. If, however, the researchers try to passively determine the path of the particles, observing them with perturbation free detectors, only two light spots are created! Even if the researchers only let one photon at a time in the experiment penetrate through the two gaps, there are several spots of light – from where does the single particle "know" that a second gap is open and how it should behave as a wave? Can one speak of "knowledge" of a quant? Because the quanta *inform* each other in some way. Is that put in an exaggerated way? The unbelievable thing is this: **This refraction of light also works with only *one* gap** (see Ill. 7 on the following pages)!

The Austrian quantum physicist **Prof. Dr. Anton Zeilinger** became known through his experiments, in which he successfully **teleported particles** for the first time. In an interview, Prof. Zeilinger remarked "Information is more fundamental than this naive concept of matter!" That means, simplified in the general sense: if you exchange the atoms of a hammer with those of a flower, it still remains the same hammer. "Just the information in the *arrangement* of the molecules characterizes the hammer, not its substance. Information is the

12 PM Online, Scheppach, Joseph, "How the forces of the cosmos determine our life", March 5, 2013

fundamental building material of this universe!" This is where another question arises: Where does this information come from? From *something* ... or just from *someone,* who informs? **The question is: How does the atom of a hammer "know" that it's not a flower atom?**
It is precisely these questions that led to the theory of "intelligent design": That the order of this universe was *"designed" by an intelligence.* And now things get even more mysterious: In theory, there shouldn't be anything in this universe that is faster than the speed of light. But there is!

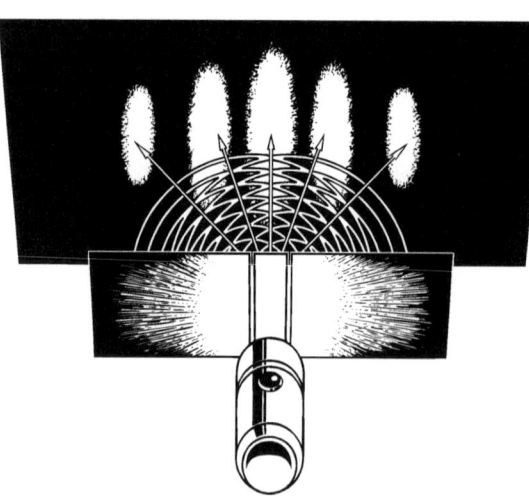

Illustration 6:
In theory there should only be two light spots on the projection screen with two splits. When a quantum is "calculated" this, too, is the only result one gets. However, with the illustration below it can be seen that several light spots form, whose structure indicates a wave characteristic.

Thus, light and quanta are "multidimensional", wave and particle at the same time.

In interviews with the physicist previously mentioned, this is also compared with the phenomenon of "duality": More precisely put, it happens in matter that at the same time has two properties. Like God who at the same time is Jesus and the Holy Spirit. And this illustrates the promises of the Bible.

This constitutes itself of all things in the evidence that the transfer of information between quanta that works at faster than light speed! (No, that doesn't mean that it will only take us a few years to get to Mars)

This phenomenon is proven in the experiment of **"entanglement"**, see illustration no. 8 on the next page: Two quanta that originated at the same time and at the same place are "related to each other". Let's take two light photons (the smileys in the illustration), which we now send through a prism, as an example. This separates their paths; they are flying apart. If one photon hits an opaque mirror, it gets "stuck" ... and at exactly the same time the other one "goes out"! If one passes through, the other one, too, continues to fly – they stay "connected" even when the mirrors are set in uneven motion. This transfer of information does not only work faster than the speed of light, but it even works without delay! This also works with other types of particles, namely electrons, atoms, atomic clouds and molecules – even beyond the gigantic distance of light years.

Is this phenomenon of Entanglement a physical proof of *reactions from God in real-time*, independent from the distance-factor maybe a prophecy for us humans, an instance of healing, an answer?
If quantum physicists want to measure the location of an electron, they can't simultaneously determine its speed. When the speed of the quantum measured,

Illustration 7:
Here a laser beam is projected through an opening onto a wall one metre away. One can clearly see the diffraction of light, the interference pattern, evidence for the fact that light quanta are matter and energy at the same time. Just like God, who is Jesus and the Holy Spirit at the same time.
Foto from the WithJesus-Team.

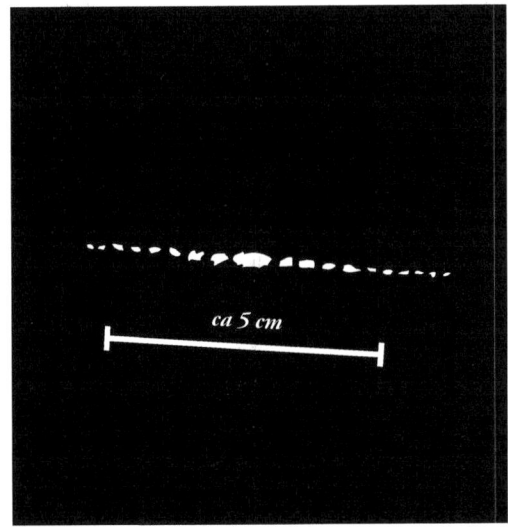

ca 5 cm

49

it cannot be localized. Einstein rumbled about it: "The moon isn't just in the sky because we're looking." **This provided proof that the quanta, from which we humans, too, can exist in *multiple* dimensions at the *same* time – they are simultaneously energy and matter.**

Prof. Zeilinger even questions **Steven Hawking's** thought as to why he did not believe in God: "An example that [note: Stephen Hawking] represented: Since we have the law of gravitation, we don't need a God who created the universe; instead the universe created itself through this law of gravitation. But exactly from this "another question has to be asked: Where does the law of gravitation come from?"[13]

And quantum physics even ascribes a potential learning ability to the universum! For the French physicist **Jean Charon** quanta are "thinking units": electrons can "eat" photons. They have a "spin", a self-rotating ability – should they ever transmit or change this spin within an electron, then the quanta would be they memory of the electron. Also a binary code would arise which, according to Monsieur Charon contains "all of the knowledge of an almighty creation!"

13 orf.at online, https://science.orf.at/stories/2901117/, 14.03.2018, from. on April 4th, 2018

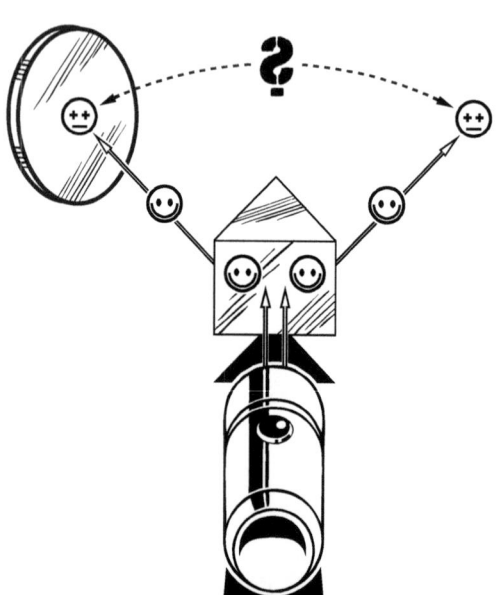

Illustration 8:
How does the one quantum (right) "know" that its "twin" has gone out?
In which way does it get this information?
Why does a transmission (symbolized by the question mark in the figure) that is faster than light, which goes against all knowledge of physics, work here?

Through this the thought of the whole universe as a morphological atomic field that stores all knowledge of all events, is conceivable and compatible with the Bible. (see p.52 point 3/5)

A member of the WithJesus-Team had a long-winded discussion on faith with a physicist for a long period of time. The physicist described himself as an atheist. But the logical arguments given by the WithJesus-Staff (which are also included in this chapter) inspired the physicist to write a small font. The title says it all: **"Soul Quanta"**©. In it the physicist describes the theoretical possibility that the soul of a human could live on in the form of a "quantum body" after the death of the human, i.e., after the death of the physically detectable body.

That would be unbelievable – please imagine this: After death we would not be bound to our forgetful brains with a limited imagination, our field of vision would not be narrowed by two eyes that become more and more farsighted in age, from our clumsy body only a quantum-body that is faster than light would remain:

Welche neuen, mehrdimensionalen Formen an Musik könnten wir dann komponieren? Welche gigantischen Licht-Bilder malen? Welche neuen Formen an Wissen, Gedächtnis, Vorstellungsvermögen oder Kommunikation hätten wir in einem Augenblick zur Verfügung?
1. Corinthians 15, Vers 44: *"... it is sown a natural body, it is raised a **spiritual** body."*

Conclusion of this chapter: The results of physics astonishingly match with many descriptions found in the Bible:

1/5) In the universe there is life – so God should also live.
The Bible describes God as the *living God* and abhors the worship of idols made of wood and stone.
Jeremiah 10ff: *"They cut a tree out of the forest, and a craftsman shapes it with his chisel. They adorn it with silver and gold; they fasten it with hammer and nails so it will not totter. [...] Their idols cannot speak; they must be carried because they cannot walk. Do not fear them [...] But the Lord is ... **the living God, the eternal king**. [...] Everyone is senseless and without knowledge; every goldsmith is shamed by his idols. The images he makes are a fraud; they have no breath in them, They are worthless, the objects of mockery!"*

2/5) God is everywhere at the same time, always, because
The prophecies of the Bible prove that *God is independent of our dimension of space and time.* Because the prophecies were verifiably written beforehand and came true afterwards! See chapter 2.2 of this book.
God is always there, waiting for us. This is confirmed in
Acts 17,27ff: *"The God who made the world and everything in it is **the Lord of heaven and earth and does not live in temples built by human hands.** And he is not served by human hands, as if he needed anything. Rather, he himself gives everyone life and breath and everything else. [...] **God did this so that they would seek him and perhaps reach out for him and find him, though he is not far from any one of us.** 'For in him we live and move and have our being.'"*

3/5) The whole universe could be one big memory:
Luke 8,17: *"For there is nothing hidden that will not be disclosed, and nothing concealed that will not be known or brought out into the open."*
Ephesians 5,11f: *"Have nothing to do with the fruitless deeds of darkness. [...] It is shameful even to mention what the disobedient do in secret. But everything exposed by the light becomes visible – **and everything that is illuminated becomes a light.**"*

4/5) There are serious physical theories to prove eternal life, which statements about life after death in the Bible confirm
Isaiah 26,19: *"But your dead will live, Lord; their bodies will rise – let those who dwell in the dust wake up and shout for joy [...] the earth will give birth to her dead."* (No, not zombies, but resurrection, see Daniel 12, 2 & 3)
John 11,25 (personal quote from Jesus): *"The one who believes in me will live, even though they die;"*

5/5) Physics allows the idea of a "spiritual world", of a multidimensional universe where God, Jesus and angels live.
We cannot yet look into this dimension with our "carnal eyes", but in the future the earth will be transformed into an eternal kingdom of peace where all people will live together with God.
Ezekiel 37,25f: *"They and their children and their children's children will live there forever. [...] I will make a covenant of peace with them; it will be an everlasting covenant. [...] My dwelling place will be with the; I will be their God, and they will be my people."*
(More information in this book, especially Chapters 2.2 and 6.3ff)

What are the findings of quantum physics?

It unintentionally reveals, explains, and affirms the nature of God: We are all a part of Him, multidimensional at the same time, since we all are made up of quanta – see illustration 1, page 19.

We are all in constant contact with God, our thoughts and prayers are transmitted without delay, regardless of any distance, which doesn't exist in the quantum cosmos.

Acts 17,28: *"For in him [note: God] we live and move and have our being'. As some of your own poets have said, 'We are his offspring.'"*

The space-time structure we are familiar with is cancelled out in quantum physics, which makes answered prayers, prophecies or the almighty, omnipresent God of the Bible more imaginable. Dimensions without time, hyperspace, or put differently "being everywhere at the same time" is not a fairy tale, but reality.

Multidimensionality is NOT "somewhere out there", instead we humans ARE multidimensionality in a multidimensional world. This is how it suddenly becomes physically imaginable that we – or our "soul quanta" – keep our memory and our individuality after our earthly death and that we can spend eternity in worship with God, something which the Bible announces in many passages!

Psalm 115,18: *" ... it is we who extol the Lord, both now and forevermore."*

Niels Bohr, Nobel Prize 1922: "If anyone is not appalled by quantum theory, then they didn't understand it."

Albert Einstein, 1926: "Quantum mechanics are very respectable ... It is absolutely possible that unexpected worlds are hidden beyond the perception of our senses!"

Professor Antoine Suarez: "The quantum ghost suggests that forces make decisions behind the visible earth, which are completely out of human control."

The famous astronomer **Carl Sagan** (who unfortunately died in 1996) is not stingy with – sorry – unproven allegations about Christians: "... instead the say 'No, no, no, my God is a small God, and I want that he stays small!' A religion, which in terms of science, emphasizes the size of the universe, could probably expect significantly more awe and reverence than traditional beliefs."[14]

Nonsense.

14 Carl Sagan, quote from his book "Pale Blue Dot"

How does Carl Sagan know that Christians want a "small God"? What kind of petty spirit is being ascribed to the Christians here once again? The Bible, Judaism, and Christianity emphasize awe, reverence, and the greatness of the universe since its existence! Here are a few samples of the **THINK BIG awareness lived among us Christians:**

Ephesians 2,7: *"In order that in the coming ages he might show the **incomparable** riches of his grace, expressed in his kindness to us in Christ Jesus."*
Ephesians 3,20: *"Now to him who is able to do **immeasurably** more than all we ask or imagine, according to his power that is at work within us, to him be glory in the church and in Christ Jesus throughout all generations, for ever and ever."*
Titus 1,2: *"In the hope of **eternal** life, which God, who does not lie, promised **before the beginning of time."***
1. John 3,20: *"We know that God is **greater than our hearts,** and he knows everything."*
Luke 9,43: *"And they were all amazed at the **greatness of God!"***
1. Corinthians 2,9: *"What no eye has seen, what no ear has heard, and what **no human mind has conceived** – the things God has prepared for those who love him."*
Job 5,9: *"He performs wonders that **cannot be fathomed, miracles that cannot be counted."*** God is infinite for Christians!

Many people believe that they can prove God's non-existence with the bad events of this world. To do this, they utilize horrible events in their personal lives and disaster news in the media as examples – see chapter 5.0 f.
Atheists often accuse Christians that being Christian prevents any kind of research. Complete nonsense, since **many scientists started doing research because of their faith or became Christians *because of* science!**
And if we didn't believe in God, then the most interesting reason for conducting research wouldn't exist, namely *the search for God Himself!*

More and more physicists, especially quantum physicists, believe in God.
Quotes from several of these famous people, who gained at least local notoriety with their intelligence (Joke :-)) were given in chapter 2,6 and will also be continued in the following:

Max Planck (1858-1947), German physicist, quantum physics:
"Since there is neither an intelligent force nor an eternal one in the whole universe ... we must accept (!) a conscious intelligent mind behind this force!"

Guglielmo Marchese Marconi (1874-1937), Italian engineer, physicist and pioneer of radio (whose radios saved many lives on the Titanic!):
"I declare with pride that I am a believer. I believe in the power of prayer. I believe not only as a devout Catholic, but also as a scientist!"

Sir Arthur Stanley Eddington (1882-1944), English astronomer and physicist:
"Modern physics necessarily leads us to God, not away from him. None of the inventors of atheism were scientists. They were all very mediocre philosophers."

Hubert Reeves, Canadian atomic and astrophysicist (* 1932) "Man is the dumbest species. He worships an invisible God and kills a visible nature without realizing that this very nature which he destroys, is the invisible God!"

Albert Einstein (1879-1955, locally known physicist, whom you should know) in letters to his Jewish physicist buddies **Niels Bohr, Max Born and Cornelius Lanczos:**
"It seems hard to look into God's cards ... quantum mechanics is very respectable. But an inner voice tells me that this is still not the real Jacob ... it hardly brings us closer to the secret of the old man. In any case, I am convinced that he does not roll the dice." (note :-): With *the old man* Einstein referred to God)
Carl Friedrich von Weizsäcker (1901-2007), German physicist:
"The first drink from the cup of science makes you atheistic, but God waits at the bottom of the cup."

Anton Zeilinger (*1945), Austrian physicist and Nobel Prize winner: "I cannot rule out God's intervention. Does the theory of evolution leave room for God? Of course! Personally, for me, there is a God ... that I can talk to." (quote 2022)

So, folks – as the Bible recommends, let's not create a picture of God for ourselves, because we cannot imagine Him anyway, it would be idle. But let's search for Him and how we can win His offers for a fulfilled life, because then we can fully receive His blessings!
It is pointless trying to prove the non-existence of God based on the admittedly often terrible events in our world, see chapter 5.0 f.

And now, something positive about Richard Dawkins, as promised in chapter 2.3 – completely unexpectedly, he defended Christianity in the face of worldwide terror, quote (please turn the page):

"As far as I know, there are no Christians who blow up buildings. I know no Christian suicide bombers. I know of no big Christian denomination, which believes that death is the penalty for apostasy. I have mixed feelings about the decline of Christianity, insofar as Christianity can be a bulwark against something worse." and "Christianity is perhaps our best defense against abnormal forms of religion that threaten the world."[15]

Hey, you atheists, are you cowardly or brave?
Then go to Christian communities and **ask about the many miracles** the people there *personally* experienced (and not heard from the media) thanks to God's help: healing miracles, healed cancer patients, healing broken marriages, restored parent-child relationships, salvation for livelihoods that almost ended under the bridge, healing of fatal injuries, even on Christian pets.
The authors of this book have experienced all of this themselves on several occasions. Jesus recommends to following to us in
Matthew 7,7: *"Ask and it will be given to you; seek and you will find; knock and the door will be opened for you!"*
What, just knock? Let's *hammer* on God's door, He's waiting for atheists too! :-)

Thank you, no further questions please, says the WithJesus-Team.

But now back to the facts. Did we think about such highly scientific matters *before* we were born? And still we experienced the incredible miracle of live and birth. Or did we, as children, ponder about quantum physics? Isn't it completely irrelevant to us whether we are made of vibrations, frequencies, strings, light or something else? All of this is sure to cause amazement and edification, but God created a world in which human are looking for relationships, love and harmony, just as God wants it with us humans.

Isn't it a lot less important to know how a cell phone works compared to calling someone with it to say, "I love you"? We were born as tiny children and were given life. And so, we too, like children, can now receive the gift of the message of eternal life: simply trusting Jesus!

---

15 gospelherald.com online, Delaney, Elizabeth: "Richard Dawkins See's Islam as a More Severe World Threat than Christianity ", http://www.gospelherald.com/articles/61356/20160112/ richard-dawkins-sees-islam-as-a-more-severe-world-threat-than-christianity.htm, January 12, 2016, down. on June 19, 2018. This quote from Dawkins comes from the atheist "Rock Beyond Belief"-Festivals 2010 in Fort Bragg, North Carolina, USA.

Matthew 18,3: *"Truly I tell you, unless you change and become like little children, you will never enter the kingdom of heaven.* **Therefore, whoever takes the lowly position of this child is the greatest in the kingdom of heaven.** *"*

WithJesus-Team-members also had many conversations with active esotericists. These conversations left us with the impression that they were permanently watering down the existence of a living God or arguing away His existence. So, God was vaguely by them referred to as, for example, "the cosmic energy", or (quote, honestly!): "Instead of God, you can too say 'T.i.l.E.', the infinite loving energy". That what many esotericists repeated after each other in a parrot-fashion (sorry we have to talk about this!), consisted of unchecked half-knowledge, mostly a mixture of
1) Buddhism, Hinduism and adulterated Christianity
2) Conspiracy murmurs about an allegedly falsified Bible
3) Attempts to mix the religions of this world together, which, from a scientific viewpoint is implausible, because they totally contradict each other. This left us, the WithJesus-Team, with the **impression that many people from the areas of esotericism and occultism seem to want to avoid their own responsibility towards God with the help of a fantasy world.**

Yet whoever openly professes their faith in the God of the Bible and His Son Jesus Christ, does not flee from responsibility, but only then commits to it: being honest, loving one's enemies, forgiving, blessing, ect.

Imagine if your beloved children or life partner would treat you, beloved readers, not as a person, with your name, but only as a biomechanical organism. And that they would only refer to you, for example, as a "beloved carbon unit", a "longed-for accumulation of several amino acids" etc. That would probably be a little strange for you. We are convinced: In this way God is alienated from people who want to philosophize away his traits as a person. Can something that does not have the traits of a person or individuality create living people and announce biblical prophecies to them which skip space and time and always apply? Very unlikely.

We humans are persons because God is a "person". Only a living God who himself is individual, conscious, alive, intelligent, personal and creative can produce just such beings: us humans! This is like a confirmation of God whom we only find in the Bible.

2.7 Further Evidence: The Bible – No, It Was Never "Forged"

Lots of conspiracy fans, atheists, people of different faiths and esotericists like to claim that the Bible has been forged. But that can be refuted logically: Firstly, one would have to define *what* was supposedly falsified or changed and, secondly, *which text should have been in its original place.* The "Bible-was-falsified-people" of course can't do *that,* which for Christians is a certain element of humour.

To be able to *scientifically* prove that the Bible was forged any person who claims this would have to show a *demonstrably unchanged* and *older original copy.* Otherwise, it will rob itself of its credibility.
Because logically further thought, in the case of a "falsified Bible", there would need to be "unchanged originals" somewhere. Then where could these "originals" be? Or were they all collected and burned? Maybe hidden in the catacombs of the Vatican? Maybe right next to the X-Files about crashed UFOs, which are now stored in Area 51, next to a few dusty Madonna reports on the end of the world and conspiracy theories about the moon landing ... let's stop this nonsense and irony, of course not!

The Bible, the "instruction manual" of Christianity, takes first place as the best documented written work of antiquity. With 5,644 ancient manuscripts, the parts of the New Testament in its original Greek preserved and another 19,000 in Latin, Ethiopian, Slavic and Armenian. In second place is Homer's "Iliad" with only 650 manuscripts[16] – but have you ever heard about the "authenticity" of the Iliad being questioned?

For other ancient texts, e.g. by Cicero, Plato, there is often not even one dozen of manuscripts. **As explained in detail in the next chapter, the Bible is historically traceable and one would almost like to say, "grown healthily" over the course of several hundred years.**

Even the accounts that were not included in all the Bibles are in the so-called **"Apocrypha"** to read. And you can find them in the well-stocked bookstores often already with the special offers in the bargain box – that is to say, they are accessible to everyone!

16 Gabriel, Mark, "Jesus and Mohammed", Resch, 1st edition 2006, p. 267

The content of the Bible is historically and chronologically conclusive and consistent, and if something were missing it would be noticed.
But it's not.

And who would want to change the Bible? Only someone, who would benefit from it, of course. But: **no people mentioned in the Bible now have an "advantage" because the content of the Bible. Who wrote the Bible? The Jews!** And hardly anyone is doing worse in the Bible than them, this includes a lot of dramatic predictions for this people due to their wrongdoings.

If people were to write a "Holy Book" themselves in their weakness, wouldn't it than be logical from them to try to portray themselves as a "God's people", whom all must obey? But that is not written in the Bible. **The authors of the Bible, the Jews with ruthless honesty recorded themselves, their history and their wrongdoings in the Bible.** *So, the Bible is one of the most honest books of the world.*

Did the "Catholic Church 'optimize' the Bible for men and discriminate women in it"? That's also not the case, on the contrary, which can be found in the letter to the
Ephesians 5,25: *"Husbands, love your wives, just as Christ loved the church and give himself up for her ..."* And how did Jesus give himself up for the church? Selfless until death! **This here is a clear call for equality!** See chapter 5.4.

The **reincarnation**, too, was not "erased from the Bible" – the whole concept of the Bible entirely contradicts the doctrine of reincarnation, that is, the idea that one is reborn in a different body or even the body of an animal after death, believed by Hindus, Buddhists and many esoteric people.

ATTENTION: The doctrine of reincarnation is not to be confused with the **rebirth in Jesus!** For a detailed explanation see chapter 4.2 & 6.0 ff.

The following facts confirm the unchanged transmission of the biblical content with 100% precision, taking place since almost 2500 years: The **scrolls** from the **Qumram Caves,** many **papyrus fragments** with biblical texts and parts of the Gospels. And not only that: Thanks to the papyrus fragments we know that the Gospels are older than we thought, that is, that they were written even earlier and thus, closer to Jesus' life than previously anticipated.

59

Numerous archaeological findings have only increased the confirmation the authenticity and the originality of the Bible and its accounts. Much more information about this in the book "Believing? Knowing!" by the WithJesus-Team.

Has the Bible copied information from other religions?
Several events found in the Bible have similarities in older religions – from a human point of view, this thought is imminent that Jews or Christians might have "copied" something here.
One example is the thing with the **Flood,** which is also mentioned in the Gilgamesch epic, a work of Akkadian and Sumerian literature from Mesopotamia. Meso... what? Who paid attention in school? :-) Mesopotamia is the two current or intermediate current land between the rivers Euphrates and Tigris, located in contemporary Iraq. Probably the oldest cultural landscape in the world.
Now, one might be tempted to say that the Bible could have copied something from older religions. But since the Bible is known as a reliable and meticulously kept historical record, let us look at the content from a scientist's point of view: Isn't it logical then that the biblical story of the Flood was not a metaphor, but an actual event, which was recorded by multiple cultures independent from each other, which in turn, confirms the credibility of the Bible more strongly? Much more information on that in the book "Believing? Knowing!" by the WithJesus-Team.

The "ascents" in the Bible – and in the other religions
Anyone who has read the beginning of the book of Acts knows that there the resurrected Jesus is lifted up into heaven. Two angels announce to the surprised disciples that *"This same Jesus, who has been taken from you into heaven, will come back in the same way you have seen him go into heaven."* In the Old Testament the prophet Elias drives into heaven in a fiery car and the prophet Daniel tells that *"... many who are asleep under the earth, will wake up ... shine... like the stars for ever and ever!"*
Ascents also occur in older religions. In ancient Egypt it was believed that the pharaohs, who were considered demigods, drove into immortality in the barque of the sun god Re – but only after the embalming of their bodies with the goal of mummification, pretty please.
An old form of expression of Hinduism is Vedism – meaning that whoever has made sufficient sacrifices during his lifetime, follows the belief that they will be brought into the "Land of the Fathers" after death.

Have you ever heard anything of the Zoroastrics, the followers of the teaching of Zoroaster? No? But you might know one, it was Freddy Mercury, the singer of the rock band "Queen". In Zoroastrianism there also exists a creator god, a diabolical adversary, angels – and one saviour, who is to come someday and bring lasting peace.

There would be many more examples of similarities, but what makes the Bible not fall into the same mixing pot countless other beliefs are in? **What is the uniqueness of the Bible?**

1/4 First of all, all of its prophecies: They are scientifically proven, have astonishing precision and still apply today. That is unique in the history of humanity, one of the most incredible miracles. See starting chapter 2.2.

2/4 The innumerable historical records that confirm the biblical content. It is manuscripts the Bible was compiled from. The New Testament has 24,633 manuscripts alone! The Bible is thus the best-documented book of antiquity, see beginning of this chapter.

3/4 The small timespan between the events and the first manuscripts, from a historical viewpoint: For example, Papyrus 52 (see fig. below) confirms, among others, that they were finalized in the year 68 n.Chr.[17] at the latest – only 30

17 Jaroš, Univ. Prof. Dr. Karl, in "Die Presse", June 14, 2021, letters to the editor

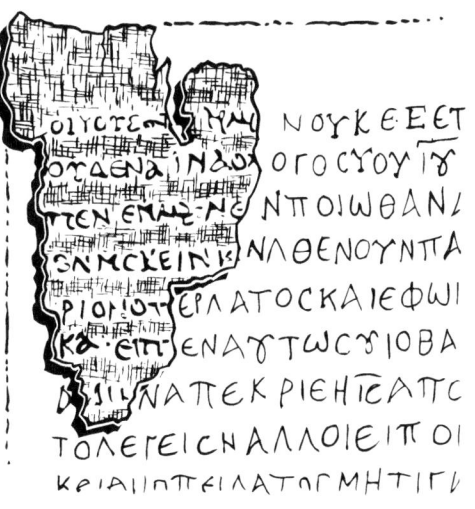

Illustration 10, Papyrus 52:
The fragment has writing on both sides and is about 6 x 9 cm big. The remaining page is indicated by dash-dotted lines and the Greek characters are written more softly.
The writing points to a non-professional clerk – all the more remarkable is the fact that the original text was preserved faithfully in the Bible.

Ⓟ©**WITH JESUS**®

61

years after Jesus' death! Science knows the compositional date of Greek and Latin reports: The oldest were written only about 750 to 1,600 years after the events!
The Bible is often questioned in the most dubious way, but less documented writings of classical antiquity are taught in schools without question.

4/4 The more than 40 (!) authors (yes, female authors too!) were able to maintain a single consistent line in their texts for 1,500 years, in three languages, spread over three continents: This applies spiritually, historically and also for the fact that they ultimately prophesied Jesus Christ, the Son of God, who actually came. Which book can claim that? The facts are clear: None. Only the Bible.

A widely debated topic on the Internet- for reasons of discretion we won't mention names here: In another religion an alleged prophet has written (with the help of his friends, due to his illiteracy) he himself claimed a "Holy Book", hundreds of years after Jesus at that. In it he claims that the "people of the book" – his term for Jews and Christians – have allegedly "changed" the Bible. However, in interviews nobody was able to explain to us, the WithJesus-Team, what was supposedly changed or what was written there instead. By the way, he is called an "alleged prophet" because nobody has been able to show a binding prophecy he had, which then came true, as the thousands of prophecies about people, cities, nations etc. found in the Bible, which verifiably came true later on.
Many believers of the religion mentioned above believe that the alleged "prophet" is "hinted at in the Bible".
Now the Christian refutation of this thought using three examples from the Bible:

Example 1/3: Envoys looking for the coming Saviour Jesus ask John the Baptist who he is – they wanted to know if he was the Christ. John the Baptist answers in the Gospel of
John 1,19-23: *"I am not the Messiah." [...] "I am the voice of one calling in the wilderness, 'Make straight the way for the Lord'"*

This does *not* mean the alleged prophet of the other religion, because John here refers to one of the 300 prophecies of the Old Testament about the Coming of Jesus, from the Bible prophet Isaiah, 40.3. Isaiah lived 740 years *before* Christ!

And if you continue reading a few lines further, John unmistakably points towards Jesus as God's Son and His work of redemption in

Johannes 1,29: *"The next day John saw Jesus coming toward him and said, 'Look, the Lamb of God, who takes away the sin of the world'"*

Believers from the other religion don't believe that because for them Jesus is not the Son of God (evidence *for* this from p.14), which is why they believe that "the Jews have falsified the Bible here". Jews and Christians refute this with documents, which prove the fact that the Bible is unchanged and are hundreds of years *older* than the Book of the alleged prophet, see page 58. The Bible exists in the form of the Codex Sinaiticus already since the year 350 AD and here, the above passage of scripture as we know it, already is written 300 years *before* the alleged prophet of the other religion. Or another example: The Qumram scrolls, see from page 25: The scroll with the book of the prophet Isaiah corresponds to today's Bible text and was written 200 years *before* Jesus – about 820 years before the alleged prophet of the other religion.

Accusation of falsification refuted – unchanged Bible confirmed!

Example 2/3, ATTENTION: Jesus announces his Holy Spirit in the New Testament for believers in

John 14,16f: *"And I will ask the Father, and he will give you another advocate to help you and be with you forever, the **Spirit of truth.** "*

In interviews believers of the other religion told us that their alleged prophet was meant by that. Because he claims in his book: "Jesus the Sohn of Mary said: 'O you children of Israel, truly I am a messenger [of the God of the other religion] who confirms the Torah [= the first five books of Moses in the Bible], which you already have received from me and I bring good news about a messenger who will come after me and whose name will be Ahmed'".

Refutation based on biblical facts:

• The New Testament is in Greek – the alleged prophet knew it.

• Ahmed is a variation of the name of the alleged prophet and is called "the praised', Greek *"perikletos"*. In the original Greek texts of the Bible but if it says *"parakletos"* (you can see the difference in the "e" and "a"), **that is the Greek term for *"spirit (!) of truth"*** that Jesus personally announced to us in the above biblical passage from John 14:16 f.

This passage definitely describes the Holy Spirit and *not* the alleged prophet. Reading tip: Acts of the Apostles, chap. 1 & 2 – a super exciting story! **Confirmation that the Bible remains unchanged!**

Example 3/3: Please read **John 14,16** again: *"And I will ask the Father, and he will give you another advocate to help you and **be with you forever** – the Spirit of truth."*
Until *forever?* Again, the Bible only means the Holy Spirit and not the alleged prophet, because this person has left us due to death.
***Anyone* who claims that "the Bible has been forged" would have to bring a *demonstrably* older *and* original copy for their credibility.
That would be the only evidence of a forged Bible.**
Accusation of falsification refuted – confirmation that the Bible is unchanged!

A doctor of theology of the other religion who became a Christian after studying the Bible created quite an uproar in the world of the other religion with a quote like this one: "These prophecies found their fulfilment independently of [the alleged prophet]. This is another indication of the lack of persuasiveness of the teaching [of the other religion] about the falsification of the Holy Scriptures."

And what about the other religions from the perspective of the Bible? One gets the impression, that almost everyone has some kind of a hunch that God exists. From a hunch a search arises, from the supposed results of this search according to our absolute conviction the different religions developed. See chapter 4.0. **But God only revealed himself through the Jews and the Bible,** the only one "Holy Book", which proves a supernatural, living God, see p. 13. Christians often get condemned and labelled as intolerant because of their thought of "exclusivity", that only Christianity is the truth. But ... what else should Christians do with *such* evidence and facts?

Nevertheless, real Christians regard those of different faiths as equal, respect other faiths and do not discriminate against anyone because of their other belief. The Bible obliges us to do so.

More on archaeological and historical evidence of biblical content can be found in the book "Believing? Knowing!" by the WithJesus-Team.

Dear reader, even if you are not a Christian, we bless you, pray for your health and for a full, happy life – may you soon have the most wonderful adventures or experience personal help for your life with Jesus, things you don't even dare to hope for.

2.8 Further Evidence: Near-Death Experiences - We Are Also Soul & Spirit

Are near-death experiences just imagination or can they be proven?
Do the brain and hormones play tricks on the dying?
Are they illusions of desperate people, the sick and those left behind?

Many people who were close to death or were clinically dead due to an illness or an accident, have had near-death experiences. The German "Near death experience-Network" reports that in Germany alone four million people are said to have had near-death experiences.[18] It would be too easy to explain these experiences with a lack of oxygen, bursts of adrenaline or psychologically exceptional reactions. Because a significant number of experiences contain demonstrable matches and demonstrable phenomena:

Why did so many people of *all* religions who were near death have the same vision of floating through a tunnel into the light or frequently seeing each other lie at the bedside, detached from their body, "from above"? And they can, although physically unconscious, remember the activities of the attending physicians as well as who was *in* the room and also often who was in *the next room!* And even people who were born blind are said to have experienced that! Children with near death experiences are said to have seen angels – and after their recovery they supposedly asked their parents why these angels didn't have wings. (If you've read the chapters on quantum physics then you know how angels can fly without wings :-)).
In the Bible it is never mentioned that angels have wings.

In near death experiences people are also said to have met their relatives, unable to explain why what they were doing "on the other side". After their "return" to life they tried to contact these relatives, but they were indeed already dead! **After near death experiences children reported to their parents that they saw a brother or a sister in heaven** – and the surprised parents had to admit that they had never told their child about its deceased siblings.

A brilliant attempt: The WithJesus-Team knows surgeons who have often heard about near death experiences from their patients. This prompted them to have an interesting idea: They wrote a legible message on a piece of paper-

18 https://netzwerk-nahtoderfahrung.org/, ab. on July 9, 2018

and put it on a spot, which was not visible from below, on the top of the large lamp in the operating room. Should a patient remember this message after an operation and after being clinically dead, then this would be the ultimate evidence! Many near death experiences could of course – theoretically – be made-up stories.

The WithJesus-Team *only* **collects and archives near-death experiences of credible people, who** *personally* **told their stories to the WithJesus-Team! Here are seven examples:**

1/7) The father of a WithJesus-Employee was never a believer and rejected the content of the Bible. Just before he died, he reported that he suddenly saw his hospital bed against the ceiling and also himself lying in it. After a moment of shock he realized that he was on the ceiling and that he saw his body *from above* in the bed *below!* That is, he had assumed that he was still lying in his bed and hadn't felt gravity. Even he, who never believed in the supernatural, had experienced being detached from his body for a short while.

2/7) Again and again it is reported that people about to die get this completely radiant look "into nothing", with a smile full of bliss, repeatedly saying things like "I can see the angels" or "Oh how beautiful, how beautiful!" with their last strength. A WithJesus-Team-Member knew an old, seriously ill man who was not a believer and was just lying in a bed of a hospice, resigned after a difficult life. He hadn't laughed in years. A few hours before his death his sister was visiting, when he suddenly sat up, with a radiant face staring into a direction where nobody was standing and reached out his hand as if he wanted to greet somebody! He sat like this for a minute or so. Shortly after he died. His sister hadn't seen him this happy in years ...

3/7) Something similar happened to the grandmother of a WithJesus-Staff: Even though she repeatedly assured that she "could not read the Bible or believe its content", she lay seriously ill in her bed at night shortly before her death, with her eyes closed, her arms stretched up in the sky for hours and her fingers wobbling as if she wanted to reach for something. The next morning, she told this very surprised, with a weak voice: "I saw a white, radiant figure floating above me, with a shining star on the forehead, which continuously held my hands all the time and comforted me!"
Who would not think of an angel here who probably wanted to accompany the elderly lady through her last hours and then to God?

4/7) *Scientific* proof of life after death?

In 2008 Dr. Just Alexander, a neurosurgeon and lecturer at Harvard University, fell ill, suffered from bacterial meningitis and fell in a coma for seven days. In his book "Proof of Heaven", 2012 he describes how he experienced different dimensions in a coma, sees flying beings who "can't help but sing with joy" and that it is difficult for him to find words for his otherworldly experience: This is similar to a chimpanzee turning into a scientist for higher mathematics for a day – and after his return to the ape dimension, he tries to describe his experiences to the other chimpanzees in monkey language.

The special thing about this book, which is not undisputed, is its appendix: There Dr. Alexander systematically, medically and logically explains that his brain was completely switched off by the inflammation and that his memories could not have been a last flare-up of the brain functions.

5/7) An example of an out-of-body near-death experience?

A best friend of a WithJesus-Staff said that he came to a terrible car accident as a medic. A seriously injured elderly couple had to be quickly rescued from a completely smashed vehicle, the man was in a coma. A few weeks later the helper met the older man in the hospital, who greeted him with a smile: "I know you, you were with us the accident, right?" Our friend was completely perplexed: How could the man recognize him even though he was unconscious and near death at the time?

Often reported, but this time from a near-death patient *personally* told to a WithJesus-Team member: A man of about 40 years of age suffered a heart attack in this young age in a pub, passed out and saw his deceased family members in the afterlife who said to him: "Your time has not yet come, you have to go back!" The man actually survived – and afterwards became a Christian because of this experience.

7/7) WARNING – evidence of the afterlife: there are many books about miracles only through prayers to Jesus, healing of the terminally ill and even the dead are said to have come back to life. **The WithJesus-Team is very careful of such reports – some are true, but also some forgeries are known to us. However, the following story is from the immediate circle of friends of the WithJesus-Staff:**

Raphaela, mother of two, lay in bed in the evening and read a (serious) book about a boy who was clinically dead after a ruptured appendix, a hopeless case

according to doctors. But his parents desperately began to pray to Jesus! Their young son woke up and got well. Raphaela started crying over the book with emotion when her eight-year-old daughter came into the room and asked about the cause of the tears. Raphaela told her about the content of the book and what the boy experienced: That he saw his parents praying in the next room, that he was carried to heaven by angels, that he there saw his deceased sister whom his parents had never told him about before his eyes, that he saw God as a gigantic light full of love and that God told him that he couldn't stay here yet.
Then the daughter replied: "I also experienced something like that, but then I was still a very little baby. I don't know if I dreamed that, it's been a long time, but angels also carried me to heaven!"

Raphaela was shocked, but the daughter told more details that were *exactly like those* in the book about the boy, which she had never read or heard about before: About a large golden staircase with an incredibly large number of angels, about many overjoyed people. Then the mother confessed to her: "You never dreamed that. You had a cardiac arrest after giving birth – You were declared dead by the doctors! I didn't want to tell you that until your 20th birthday." And then she asked her daughter the biggest question: "Did you see God too?" And the daughter replied, "Yes!" and described God as a living source of unbelievable, never seen light and colours, supernatural music and infinite love! Shortly afterwards, she painted a picture in school of how she imagined heaven: Yellow rays of warm light and everything full of hearts and music ...

Dear Sir or Madam, is this story not evidence for the existence of heaven because it came from a *completely unaffected,* newborn child?
The parents didn't know anything about a golden staircase or all the other details back then, didn't talk to their daughter about the book or about the reanimated boy. They never even spoke with someone who had a near-death experience, if you can still speak of a "near"-death here. And such stories are collected by the WithJesus-Team.

Does the soul have weight? Since 1907, scientists have been discovering inexplicable weight loss of up to 69 grams at the moment of clinical death of humans (and even animals), after precision scales had been connected to the beds of the dying. Even if the psychostasis (the technical term for this) according to researcher Len Fisher[19] has provided "no satisfactory explanation" yet:

19 Fisher, Len, "The Attempt to Weigh the Soul, and Other Great Hours ...", p. 29-35

Thanks to Albert Einstein we know that energy also has mass, and the difference in weight of the dying was clearly measured – could it actually have been the soul that left the dying body?

IMPORTANT – an "unfashionable" remark of the WithJesus-Team: Since people of all religions have noticeably similar near-death experiences, one could say that "every religion leads to God". But that's not a finished thought, there is a more purposeful *and* logical statement in the end:

Because the near-death experiences of believers of all religions resemble each other so much, it is possible that there *can only be one "true religion",* whose "actuality" every person will personally experience after their death at the latest. One thing is certain: there must be "something" or "more". There is more than enough evidence that science cannot explain.
The Bible can explain.

How you can feel that you have soul & spirit ©
This experiment is intellectual property of the
WithJesus-Team

Please close your eyes for a moment and imagine ... let's say a dog. You now see the dog – but not with your "carnal" eyes. So you have a **"projection surface"** in your brain, but also an **"observation Position"**. Some also call this "head cinema" (see fig. no. 10 next page). The projection surface can still be explained somehow: Rays of light cast an image of an object onto your retina, the visual nerve transported the image to the brain and there it was stored. But what about the "observation position"? Which department of your brain "sees" this idea in your brain? How can *you see,* what is *stored in you?* Why can your "I" "see" independently of your body?
Oops ... that won't be your soul, will it?
Or can this phenomenon be explained medically and physically?

So the WithJesus-Authors interviewed a doctor of psychiatry. She explained: "In magnetic resonance therapy you can see *what* people are *imagining* in their heads: e.g. something visual or something acoustic. Even if a person does not see or hear anything at the moment, the visually or acoustically responsible region in the brain visibly active. However, the 'observation position' can, at best, only be explained psychologically – it depends on the age of a person. For

example, a baby itself cannot reflect, only in the course of infancy can it reflect on its mother. Later the ability of self-awareness increases too. However, the 'observation position' is physically and medically not explicable! **We can only conclude that the human being is a unity of body, mind and soul."**
Hey guys, that's what a psychiatrist says! And that's what the Bible says too ...

This raises the question: Where in the human being is "the I", which can look at, smell, hear, etc. these projections or memories? Somewhere the body *must* actually be connected to a soul.
Obviously, the human being is a multidimensional being that is not just made up of his own body. And no brain researcher can explain these facts completely.
Humans are not just "meat" – even medical professionals say: The human is a unity of body, soul and spirit! That's what the Bible says too.
The ancient Greek culture sees the human being rather "binary", with a "lower and ephemeral" body and a "sublime and eternal soul".
The Bible says more holistically that the person "is" a body, "is" a soul and "is" a spirit. The spirit is the spark of life of God, which separates the Living from the Dead.

The soul is the seat of needs, is called in Hebrew "Näfäsch", ie "throat" in the sense of "thirst" = need. If one does not know God, one "clogs" the soul as a substitute with earthly needs, but one of whose weight one can become free

Illustration 10: That you can "remember or imagine something", e.g. a dog, seems to happen without question for most people. But try to realize the miracle and make yourself aware that you can look at your memories or ideas in your head (!) – like one a cinema screen: head cinema!
That is unbelievable and with cannot be explained "with just a body". That is only possible because man is also soul and spirit, thus a "subtle matter". And according to the Bible, this lives on forever.

70

through faith in Jesus and through eternal life which is connected to that. That doesn't mean that one should be mindless – Christians are also allowed to be happy about a working car, a great vacation and fulfilled love with the spouse enjoy (yes yes, this too – if you understand :-)). In the case of the death the body dies, but spirit and soul go to God, even Jesus said this, just before he died on the cross, in

Luke 23,46: *"Father, into your hands I commit my spirit!"*

The Bible mentions the "heart" even more often than "soul" and "spirit"!
Eze 36,26: *"I will give you a new heart and put a new spirit in you!"* says God *to us personally!*

The Bible says: people do not "have" soul or spirit, but *"are"* soul and spirit! So, God "is" Spirit too: The Holy Spirit. Here too not as a component, but in the sense that God "in His function" as the Holy Spirit, for example, can inspire us, heal us, build us up and much more.

Some claim that humans are biochemical mechanisms like a car battery: the function of small biomechanical power plants is comparable with the well-known attempt to connect **potatoes** (= potatoes, see illustration below) in sequence with cables in order to get a lightbulb to light up – it really works. But will such a mechanism, only a bit more complex than a human, without impulse from outside, as a human ever multiply, compose operas or calculate

Illustration 11:
Various metals, bases and acids in the potatoes provide the energy to the one small lamp for luminescent th bring.
But even if you theoretically this mechanism too a quantum computer enlarged, can from it an individual with ego Become conscious? Barely. People are more than Bio-mechanisms!

71

the speed of light? Most likely not. Just because a biomechanical apparatus becomes more complex doesn't mean that it will "automatically" develop a soul or an "I-consciousness". Will this "apparatus" not only *re-act* but also *act,* be creative, playful, recognize itself, be artistically active or even selfless like Jesus? Hardly ...

We're not biorobots like the monster from the famous movie "Frankenstein". God put His attributes in us:

Genesis chap. 1, verse 27: *"So God created mankind in his own image, in the image of God he created them; male and female he created them."*

At some point, the cells of the human body were "programmed" to have some sort of expiration date. With every cell division, the chromosome-DNA gets slightly shorter at the end, after 40 divisions it is over for most cells. After Adam became 930 years old, Metuschelach (better known as "Methuselah") even lived to be 969, his son Lamech regrettably died comparatively young at only 777 years, God limited the age of the humans to 120. The pension funds of this world are groaning! :-)

According to the latest scientific discoveries, a person can live to be around 120 years old – science thus confirms a quotation from the Bible found in **Genesis 6,3:** *"Then the Lord said, 'My Spirit will not contend with humans forever, for they are mortal; their days will be a hundred and twenty years.'"*
The *verifiably* oldest person was the French woman Jeanne Calments, who died in 1997 – she was 122 years old![20]

Amazing, how the Bible again and again anticipates modern discoveries of science ...

2.9 What is the Bible?
The entrance to the greatest adventure!

The Bible is the "operating manual" of Christianity, for Christians it is **"normative",** that is, God's word and truth. "Truth" ... an inflated term and controversial concept taken by the religions of our world. And their critics prefer to use it even more – as a projection surface for their emotions?

20 n-tv Online, "Life Expectations", https: //www.n-tv.de/mediathek/bilderserien/wissen/ Life expectancies-article7263516.html, 11.8.2016, down. on March 21, 2018

But in contrast to all (and really all) other more or less "holy books", the Bible can scientifically prove its supernatural origins. See from chapter 2.2

Should you, dear reader, have only entered the book here and also, just like many other people, think that the content of the Bible has been changed: **The content of the Bible was never rewritten, but always remained the same.** This can be traced back to many archaeological findings of biblical writings that are hundreds, actually thousands of years old, e.g. the Qumran scrolls and many papyrus findings. See chapters 2.5 and 2.7.

Where does the term "Bible" come from anyway? From the Phoenician port city of Byblos, from which Greeks took over the letters of our alphabet from Canaan in the 9th century BC.
Byblos, on the other hand, means "papyrus bush" or "papyrus bast": In antiquity the city was the main hub for bast, the raw material for production of paper rolls on which the Bible was written down over time.

A few (almost :-)) unknown facts about the Bible:
The Bible is the most printed, the most translated, and the most extensively spread book to the world.
The Bible became complete in 475 languages and was partly translated in 2538 languages! Five billion copies of the Bible have been sold to date. Another 100 million copies are currently produced each year.
But one of the least known facts is: the Bible was written entirely by Jews. And that confirms the truthfulness of the Bible in a bizarre way. Because although the Jews are the "people of God" in it – did they set a memorial with the Bible or took advantage of its content? No! Because in it they describe with amazing honesty their failure, their falling away from God and the consequences thereof, all the way to dramatic predictions for future events.
The Bible is therefore one of the most honest books in the world.

And this incredible announcement about the Jews comes from Jesus himself:
John 4,21: *"Jesus replied ... We worship what we do know, for salvation is from the Jews".*

There are two major religions that believe in the contents of the Bible: Jews and Christians. Muslims have only limited faith in the Bible because they think it was falsified by "the people of the scriptures" = Jews and Christians, but do not say where and what should have been written there. This is incomprehensible for most Christians. Info and far too little-known facts about this in Chapter 2.7.

Jews, Christians and Muslims are referred to as the "Abrahamic Religions", since all three of them refer to the ancestor Abraham.
The Bible is a chronologically and thematically arranged collection of reports ("books"*, Gospels, letters, more about that in a moment), whose content has been compiled for almost 3000 years. This compilation is called "canon", which is Latin and means something like "benchmark" or "guideline". With the expression *"Books of the Bible" the different chapters of the Bible are meant, for example "The Book of Isaiah" about the prophet Isaiah.
The Bible can first be divided into two broad areas:

• The **Old Testament** (to be abbreviated as **"OT"** from now on) talks about the time before the Life of Jesus Christ. It was made almost entirely in Hebrew, based on small parts written in Aramaic, but written not in the Hebrew, but in the then more respected ancient Phoenician alphabet.
The process of canonicalization took place in a fascinating dynamic for the first part of OT, the five books of Moses were completed as early as 400 BC. Christ, the rest of the OT approx. 200 BC Christ.

• The **New Testament** (abbreviated to **"NT"** in the future) talks about the time from the birth of Jesus Christ. It was written in Greek colloquial language. In the OT and NT however, there are short parts written in Aramaic, the mother tongue of Jesus. The so-called **"square script"** each letter fit into a square of the same size originated from Aramaic – they are the Hebrew characters that are still known and valid today!

The finished canonization of the NT was confirmed at the latest in 367 AD by the Bishop **Athanasius of Alexandria** confirmed in his 39th Easter letter. He lists the 27 books of the NT that are still recognized today by all Christian churches. Even **Pope Gelasius I** (492-496) confirmed in his "Dekretum Gelasianum" the finished content and cites additional writings, the **"Apocrypha"** (more about that in a moment).
To put it simply, the Jews only believe in the OT, since they do not see Jesus as the Son of God or as the Messiah. They believe that the Messiah has yet to

come. For Christians, the New Testament is the good news of God and His Son Jesus, however for Jews, it is "not valid". From a scientific and logical viewpoint, the content of the NT is confirmed through the numerous prophecies and announcements in the OT.

Warning: The Bible of the Jews and the Old Testament of the various Christian denominations (Catholic, Protestant, Orthodox etc.) are the same in principle, but the order of the content varies a little.

The Apocrypha: some churches (Orthodox, Catholic, Slavic etc.) also have a few additional, "supplementary" books and in their Bibles. Jews and the Protestants Bible versions do *not* contain these writings. These supplementary books are called "apocryphal" by Jews or by Christian denominations, who did *not* include them in their Bibles. This term comes from the ancient Greek "apo-kryphos"= "hidden". In general, these books are also called "The Apocrypha".

Important information for "friends" of conspiracy: the Apocrypha *do not* contain secrets or hidden information, which members of secret societies, Freemasons, Illuminati and the Vatican (nonsense, of course not, end of irony :-)) want to keep away from us. Also, the Apocrypha are not hidden in secret dungeons of the Vatican but can be obtained legally by everyone in the bargain boxes of well-sorted bookshops.

Here is a story about the supernatural power of the Bible: A few years ago a WithJesus-Staff was in bed on an early Sunday morning, next to him his sleeping wife and decided to switch up his Bible reading rhythm from this day onwards: He thought: "From now on, so that every day and every night will be sealed with the Word of God, I will read the Bible every morning, as soon as I wake up and every evening, as close as possible before sleeping!"
But in *the very moment* when he *thought* about the word "Bible" his wife clearly said the word "Bible" *in her sleep*! Our staff first thought that his wife wanted to tease him – but she couldn't even have known what he was thinking even if she had been awake and kept on sleeping.
This was a greeting *and* a confirmation from heaven!

Much more information about this in the book "Believing? Knowing!" by the WithJesus-Team.

3.0 Christianity Isn't a Sect, Isn't "Esoteric", Isn't a "Religion", Isn't a "Philosophy", But ..

... Christianity is practiced charity, a binding commitment to take over responsibility for forgiveness and help. Christianity is a restoration of contact of people with God through His Son Jesus.
Yes, it works. No, we don't do drugs.   :-)

What do the frequently used terms "esotericism", "religion" etc. even mean?

Esotericism and occultism are becoming more and more socially acceptable: Reasonable people suddenly shape their lives according to astrological principles, managing directors consult clairvoyants, seemingly down-to-earth people conduct their interior design according to the decisions of diviners and pendulum experts and end up placing the double bed in the built-in wardrobe, so that "negative vibrations" don't rob them of their sleep or health. Educated people attend seminars to travel out of their bodies ... can one also learn how to find your way back into your body in these seminars? :-)

The bad thing is that esotericism and occultism dilute the message of Jesus, by dismissing it as "just one of many perspectives", as "just one of many other paths in the search of enlightenment" – that does not match the facts. Because most people don't know that the Bible is the only book, which proves itself in a supernatural manner. See from Chapter 2.0, if you haven't read it yet.

We as Christians from the WithJesus-Team don't look at these "exotic" beliefs, such as esotericism, occultism and the increasingly popular "old pagan beliefs" in a sceptical manner because of intolerance, but because after close research we have discovered real dangers and consequences behind their facade: Practising esotericists in the immediate vicinity of the WithJesus-Team became very ill, physically and mentally, fell into depression; families and marriages broke apart, livelihoods failed, even instances of suicide happened due to a complete loss of realism.

We see it as our responsibility to warn against this!
Instead of conducting a theoretical analysis of different areas, we will now look at several actual cases that occurred in the vicinity of the WithJesus-Team. These cases or practical examples are symptomatic for esoteric and occultism and come from the research done by the WithJesus-Team for almost 40 years. We will also compare esotericism and occultism with biblical passages.

In Latin, **religion** means "religio" = "conscientious care in observance of signs and rules".
Christianity is therefore not "religious" and needs neither rules nor laws, but is ... see above left under the heading.

Esotericism in ancient Greek means "esoterikos" = "inner", belonging to an "inner area" or "only accessible to an inner, specific group of people".
Occultism in Latin means "occultus" = "hidden", "covered", "secret", "esoteric", "paranormal", "mystical" or "supernatural".

**This is what *Paul* says on the subject of "secretly" or "hidden" in the
2. Letter to the Corinthians 4,2:** *"Rather, we have **renounced secret and shameful ways** [...] nor do we distort the word of God. On the contrary, by setting forth the truth plainly we commend ourselves to everyone's conscience in the sight of God."*
Ephesians 5,12f: *"Have nothing to do with the fruitless deeds of darkness, but **rather expose them**. It is shameful even to mention what the disobedient do **in secret.**"*
**This is what *Jesus* says on the subject of "in secret" and "hidden" in
Matthew 10,26:** *"So do not be afraid of them, for there is nothing concealed that will not be made known."*

Important: God advises clearly in many places in the Bible of every kind of secrecy. From several conversations with esotericists or occultists we know that a significant number of them due to their "knowledge" view themselves – sorry – as something "better" or "more developed" than their fellow human beings and position themselves above them – Jesus' opinion on that can be found in
Matthew 23,12: *"For **those who exalt themselves will be humbled,** and those who humble themselves will be exalted."*

What is important now is the meaning of the following terms:
mental: relating to the human spirit, Greek "psyche"
spiritual: spiritual, also including the supernatural

Pseudosciences have become a global industry. Pseudoscientists lie to us – and to themselves? – on a gruesome way, because in the best case one experiences subjective experiences with which one can, however, fool oneself admirably. Example:

Ever seen **dowsers** on their search for treasure and water veins? The German **"Society for Scientific Investigation of Parasciences"** could after most detailed investigations not detect any significant deviations from expected random hits. Even so, many people spend unbelievable sums of money for esoteric services or articles: e.g. only 4,400 $ for an approx. 1 meter (= 3 feet 3 3/8 inches) high column made of copper pipes, with a small glass pyramid mounted on top, in which coloured pebbles were poured, which should be able to do the unbelievable: "Environmental pollution from chemtrails are brought into harmony, ether fields of the sky are brought back into balance and life energy is accelerated".
"Energy pads made of 0,28 inches satined plastic", approx. as big as a kitchen tile, if placed on the floor in corners will lift the "life energy level of the enclosed rooms up to a life-promoting and constructive level" and "keep out earth rays": only $ 125,- per piece. When hung on the body, the pads are supposed to be "a space for transformation and protection form, which supplies vital energies". A wire spiral like the one on grandpa's desk where one can put letters in, can, if hung around the neck, keep "negative vibrations out and bring us in tune with cosmic rhythms". No serious science could ever prove any effect of such pseudoscientific products![21]

Wait – and what about the praying Christians? Can you prove the effects when Christians pray? Yes, you can! More information in chap. 2.3.

One thing needs to be said very clearly about esotericism and occultism and their practical implementation: Attention! Stay away! Hands off!

---

21 Youtube.com, Lesch, Harald, "Terra X Lesch & Co – Wie Pseudowissenschaftler uns belügen", https://www.youtube.com/watch?v=FjfoNLaE1Hc&spfreload=5, 18.10.2017, abger. am 2.12.2017

3.I Jesus - or Esotericism, Occultism, Fortune Telling, Astrology, Philosophie?

Example 1: Jesus or Esotericism and Occultism?
A 34-year-old "new" Christian known to the WithJesus-Team was confronted with a challenging question by a fan of esotericism: "If only the Christian way is supposed to be the truth, why do esoteric healing methods sometimes help? Why do self-proclaimed clairvoyants often 'know' things they can't know? Why do occult rituals 'work', although God does not want that according to the Bible?" Since the interviewee was still an inexperienced Christian, he could not answer this question immediately. So, in the evening he prayed and asked God for an answer: What should he say to the friend? After his prayer our Christian helplessly and without a plan opened up the Bible "somewhere random" and began to read:

Deuteronomy 13,1f: *"If a prophet, or one who foretells by dreams, appears among you and announces to you a sign or wonder,* **and if the sign or wonder spoken of takes place,** *and the prophet says, 'Let us follow other gods' (gods you have not known) 'and let us worship them', you must not listen to the words of that prophet or dreamer.* **The Lord your God is testing you to find out whether you love him with all your heart and with all your soul."**

God, through his Word, the Bible, led our young Christian to the answer that is: God sometimes lets these signs and wonders of esotericists, shamans, card readers etc. happen – so that God and we (!) know what we have chosen. **All too often, wishes fulfilled through esotericism and the like have worse consequences than if the "wish" had not been fulfilled in the first place. We only get real blessings when we entrust our needs to God – He gives us what we really need, see chap. 2.4.**

A popular phrase used by esotericists is that "every person brought themselves to the world" – which is supposed to suggest that there is no God and especially not the One of the Bible. Our answer to that: Then you would have to kill yourself and then bring "yourself" back into the world, right? This always results in an embarrassed silence from the esoteric ... please *don't* try!!

Example 2: Christian prophecy or the neighbour's fortune teller?
1 Corinthians 14,3: *"But the one who prophesies speaks to people for their strengthening, encouraging or comfort."*
Every Christian can get a prophecy from God. For yourself, for the friend, for

family members, a colleague or for the neighbours who love to argue ... more info in chapter 2.4 and from chapter 6.0 of this book.

A prophecy should be *positive* and *edifying* for the recipient, then it comes more from God and not from one's own emotions.
Prophecies with *negative* content show what the "spiritually opposite side" wants to do with you (see chapters 5.3 and 5.4 of this book).
Negative prophecies can be easily "broken" and it works like that – sounds absurd to outsiders, but it works: you just say **"I am breaking the statement that this or that** (accident, Illness, etc.) **should happen to me in Jesus' name! I set myself** (or other people) **free in Jesus' name!"** An elderly friend of a WithJesus-Writer said that an esoteric fortune teller in a tavern predicted the divorce of his marriage, which then came true. Of course, the poor man now believes that all of these fortune tellers have psychic abilities.

A Christian would have averted this negative prophecy, and it goes like this:
1/3 "In Jesus' name break" the statement of the fortune teller of the failure of the marriage *as soon as possible* in prayer, if possible with a second person.
2/3 If possible, naturally pray with your spouse! In any case pray *for* the spouse, marriage and love...
3/3 Couples mostly have loved each other so much, otherwise they would not have gotten married. In the event of a crisis in the marriage, the most important thing is to pray together: Together ask God to renew your first love, then forgive one another, reconcile and / or seek counselling together, but not an esoteric, but a Christian one!
Our recommendation:
Never **go to a fortune teller or clairvoyant again and warn the people in your surroundings about it!** If the above mentioned older friend of the author had instead practiced the recommendations of the Bible, he would most likely still with his wife – and happier than before.
This is what God personally tells us about divination about the prophet Isaiah 8,19: *"When someone tells you to consult mediums and spiritists, who whisper and mutter, should not a people inquire of their God? Why consult the dead on behalf of the living?"*
(For the credibility of the prophet Isaiah, please read chapter 2.5 of this book: In 700 BC Isaiah had foretold that in one day Israel would arise again – against all expectations that came true on May 14, 1948 – only one of thousands of Bible prophecies that have come true! See Isaiah 66,8)

Example 3: Astrology

Astronomy Greek "astron" = "star" and "nómos" = "law".

Astrology Greek "astron" = "star" and "logos" = "knowledge".

Astronomy is serious research; astrology is esoteric half-knowledge – the difference should be clear ... :-)

Peoples of past millennia, especially Greeks and Arabs, were fascinated with the constant figures of the fixed stars. At some point they connected the stars into shapes and interpreted figures: ibexes, cancers, dogs, virgins ... and if the ever-wandering planet Venus (or another planet) was in the constellation of the rabbit (just one example, please no splitting hairs :-)) and there was war, one thought there would be war again whenever Venus approached the rabbit.

Yes, unfortunately the principle of astrology is so simple ... ok, maybe a little more complex, but that's how it works. Who is born under which star and when? Perhaps, according to astrology, a person is of a warlike nature, because at the time of his birth Venus was back in the constellation of the rabbit ... end of irony.

Astrology crops and distorts one of the most precious gifts God gave to the people: free will!

The people in spoiled industrialized countries are admittedly primarily concerned about their personal freedom, but millions of people read the horoscopes frequently found in dubious newspapers every day and orient their lives according to astrology: when cutting fingernails, when cleaning the windows, at interview appointments, when choosing sexual partners. Try to get an appointment at the hairdresser's on "Leo" or "Virgo days" – almost impossible, since many people believe that their hair becomes more beautiful when cut on these days. And on "Capricorn days" the hair becomes unruly and difficult to comb. And only because some planet is positioned in front of a few stars which reminded someone of a lion or a virgin a few thousand years ago! A member of the WithJesus-Team used to work for a newspaper and knows that most of the horoscopes are only ... *invented...* by female journalists during their coffee gossip with much giggling!

Astrology ingeniously exposed: The **Serial Killer Experiment** of the French psychologist **Michel Gauquelin** refutes even "professional" astrology:

In 1968 Gauquelin gave "very personal horoscopes" to 150 people. 94% recognized themselves in it, 90% found it "very suitable". Tricked: Actually, *all people got the same horoscope* – created by a professional astrologer for the exact dates of birth ... of a serial killer!

Countless reputable studies (including from universities) confirm that **astrology not working.** That is why we spare ourselves the source of references here, if you want, you can find a lot of them under "Astrology" on Wikipedia. Nazi greats such as SS chief Heinrich Himmler put their responsibility about life and death on astrologers and "brown magic" – we know the *"fruits of their work"* (a term used by Jesus personally).

This is what God says personally about astrology:
Jeremiah 10, 2&3: *"This is what the Lord says: Do not [...] be terrified by the signs in the heavens [note: stellar constellations], though the nations are terrified by them. For the practices of the peoples are worthless."*
Isaiah 47,13: *"Let your astrologers come forward, those stargazers who make predictions month by month, let them save you from what is coming upon you. Surely, they are like stubble; the fire will burn them up. They cannot even save themselves from the power of the flame."*
Attention, important information: In biblical accounts about the end times, we read about the **"blood moons"**, a biblical term for new moons. This has nothing to do with astrology. Because astrology is nebulous interpretation, but blood moons are dates when you can expect God to act again.

Here are four ghostly incidents from practice, which people close to the WithJesus-Team have experienced with astrology and clairvoyance:
1/4: An esoterically active man known to the WithJesus-Team fell in love and took a look at an astrology guide in order to find out what was reported about the constellation character of his wife. To his great surprise he found very precise descriptions of the nature of the young lady which seemed like a factual report from her life. He trusted the book – yet the relationship failed, nevertheless. Three years later he became a Christian, remembered this incident and became insecure: On the one hand, the Bible advises to stay away from astrology, yet on the other hand the astrology book he had consulted back then contained "correct" information! And so, he again looked at the same passage in the book and ... wasn't able to find it anymore! This is how we are letting ourselves be manipulated by astrology, esotericism and the likes – God warns us about this in the Bible, for example through the prophet
Isaiah 19, 3&14: *"Then the spirit of the Egyptians will become exhausted within them and emptied out; And I [note: God] will confuse their strategy, so that they will consult the idols and the spirits of the dead. [...] The Lord has mixed a spirit of distortion within her [...] As a drunken man staggers in his vomit."*

Isaiah 44,25: *"I am the Lord* [note: God] *[...] who foils the signs of false prophets and makes tools of diviners, who overthrows the learning of the wise and turns it into nonsense."*

2/4: A Christian engineer, also known to the WithJesus-Team, was invited to a (literally) "cool event" that would throughout the evening reveal itself as a satanic mass. But this event didn't take place during the Middle Ages or in a jungle, it happened in a European capital only a few years ago! When the conductor of the mass wanted to start his rituals on stage, calling out for Satan, he suddenly stopped and became uneasy. The visitors became curious and suddenly he stopped what he was doing and make the following announcement through the microphone: "Satan can't come, we can't follow through with the ritual, as there is a Christian among us!" The engineer felt a little queasy, since it quikkly became apparent that he was a newbie in the event. Thank God nothing happened to him, but he was asked: "How can you have so much power that you can keep Satan from coming?" The engineer responded: "I'm not the one stopping him – Jesus is doing that!"
On the way home, the engineer was attacked by a few men who waved their knives in front of his face. When the engineer meekly said, "Ok, if you want to kill me, then I will at least be faster with God." What was the reaction of the gangsters? They turned around and walked away with amazed faces ... fact!

3/4: The WithJesus-Team heard about an exceptionally talented young guitarist who was interested in esotericism and composed his music according to numerical and mystical laws – and ever since then he had been battling severe psychological problems, including a stay at a closed psychiatric ward. Some time later the young musician was declared as healed, discharged and introduced to us: Bloated from the medication he was taking, with an empty, creepy eye expression and a strangely raised voice he told us about his stay at the sea: "... I was standing at the shore... and then I saw them coming... ships, with wonderful lights..." Upon inquiry, he confirmed our worst fears: He thought he had seen UFOs. A few days later the WithJesus-Team learned that the young guitarist couldn't bear his psychological state anymore and that he had jumped in front of a train.

4/4: A young man in the vicinity of the WithJesus-Team experienced a difficult crisis with his girlfriend when he gave his life to Jesus – because his girlfriend didn't want to know anything about Jesus. Still, the young lady wanted to save the relationship and consulted a clairvoyant, highly respected in her field, against the urgent pleas of her boyfriend. When the young lady returned home, she told him that the clairvoyant saw "no wedding, but also no break-up". But the young man felt that his girlfriend didn't tell him the whole story. Months after their break-up he asked the young lady again and she confessed that the clairvoyant knew right away, which professions both of them had, that their break-up was imminent, that the man would move out and that she would get into a new relationship. Then the clairvoyant suddenly was quite surprised that she (literally) could not "say anything about the young man from this point onwards, as she was not getting any information about him- that has never happened to her, she couldn't explain what was happening."

But the WithJesus-Team can explain it: The clairvoyant got her information from the – sorry, plain language – "dark" side of the "spiritual world", in which unfortunately not angels but demons live. (More info about this from chapter 5.4 of this book). So, she couldn't see anything about him from the moment where he became a Christian and who becomes a Christian is hidden from the guys with the horns and from demons – under God's protection! This is also confirmed by Paul in his letter to the

Colossians 3,3: *"... your life is now hidden with Christ in God."*

Occultism poses a particular danger to children. Let alone celebrating **Halloween:** It stems from ancient occult rituals with which ghosts are called from the underworld. Sometimes even human sacrifices were made or bone fires were lit. "Bonfire" stems from Bonefire = *bone* fire. Honestly, can *you* explain why ...

... kids are running around at night with demonic masks on their faces on Halloween, smearing houses and cars, which their fellow humans have worked very hard for, just because they need to get *even more* candy, than they already have?

The WithJesus-Team offers an alternative to this: Children could instead dress up as angels on Halloween and bring sweets to the poor and lonely people, the single widows in their neighborhood or the elderly, bedridden people in houses for old or poor people.

Crime and murder increasingly appear in many computer games or youth films. Faces are twisted with harshness; female figures often wear clothes resembling prostitutes. Again and again, you see characters that leave the impression of being "demonized" behind. The finale in films and play is mostly "the big brawl" between the main actors and conveys that only the physically strongest count in the world. Pedagogically valuable right? Sad irony, end.

The movie cult around the poor young sorcerer's apprentice, who finds his fulfilment in a parallel world in which he is trained as a magician in a magic castle is done very cleverly: The first book and its film play in childhood of the main actor, in which neither personality nor the child's thinking are consolidated. In the sequels of the books the boy and his friends reach puberty.

Perfectly designed to accompany and influence the young readership till adulthood – because the volumes correspond to the educational levels an English boarding school. Somewhat alarming for most Christians, is the fact that meanwhile extremely wealthy author of these books, herself said that she had been inspired by the "communication with a spirit" to write this book and was accepted into the Order of the British Empire as an officer for this purpose.[22]

Why are esotericism and occultism massively on the rise in our seemingly rational and "reasonably" thinking world?
Many people lack in the performance society of the industrialized countries and the pressure it creates something all too human: warmth, comfort, and things that make life more colourful, exciting and harmonious. Esotericism deceptively creates a quickly accessible parallel world; the bill is presented later: One is often deceived and taken advantage of, sometimes financially or even sexually abused, by self- appointed miraculous healers, gurus or con men.

There is no such thing as "white" or "good" magic – ***both*** come from the guy with the horns and his demons, see chap. 5.4.

Now in simple English:
Esotericism and watered-down black magic have come as far as to even be **established in schools, while the Number 1 Sign for selfless love, The Cross, is being removed from more and more classrooms around the world.**

Sorry, but esotericism, occultism and exotic beliefs ultimately do not bring about improvement in life, but distortion: they distract from the demonstrable miracle of Jesus and the Bible.

---

22 factum magazine in jesus.ch online, Berger, Klaus Rudolf: "Sorcerer's apprentice Harry Potter", http://www.jesus.ch/magazin/jugend/youthmag/entertainment/104101-zauberlehrling_ har- ry_potter.html, 25.03.2002, ab. on June 23, 2018

Christianity Is NOT a Philosophy

Hey, what does the "love of wisdom" (that's the meaning of the Greek term "philosophy") have to do with esotericism and conspiracy theories?
We only want to go into it very briefly here, and first of all look at natural philosophy, one of the many spectra of philosophy. Because this area of philosophy, put in simple terms, searches for findings, where natural sciences, such as biology and theoretical astrophysics reach their empirical, i.e. measurable and tangible limits. A logical and neat thing.
Without wanting to generalize too much now, it is widely known, that many of the well-known philosophers came from Greek culture. As mentioned in chap. 2.8, the Bible describes humans holistically: The human is also a body, is a soul, is a spirit, something which was even confirmed for the WithJesus-Team by doctors from the fields of Neurology and Psychiatry (see page 69). In contrast, we can rather find a duality of a "lower value body" and a "higher value" soul. Maybe you can already notice it, the most important aspect of the human being is missing here: The spirit, "pneuma" in Greek, "ruach" (transliterated), God's breath of life, in Hebrew.

Several interviews by the WithJesus-Team with philosophers – please understand – have left behind an impression of illogical dissensions, which have been elevated to a certain culture- yet barely contain any answers or solutions.

Three classic claims of philosophers REFUTED:
1/4 In an interview with us, philosophers criticized the Catholic Church without further reason, calling it a "catastrophe". We responded with the following counterargument "everywhere where there are people, bad things also happen – but the Catholic Church also does a lot of good things!" to which a philosopher with a thoughtful smile replied: "Well, and what exactly is good?". Our answer to that "e.g. offering help in illness, for existential or emotional needs, imparting dignity, edifying one another or saving lives" was acknowledged with an equally smug-looking grin by the philosopher, "And who says that it is good to save lives?"
REFUTATION:
Our philosopher did not know what "the good" was, but generally condemned the Catholic Church as "catastrophic". Even though – we are certainly convinced – Catholic Christians have saved more lives than philosophers.

A refugee in distress in the Mediterranean could quickly explain what "the good" is! This creates the impression that many philosophers are unfamiliar with the world! We *are* alive now. And this must be mastered. Even if we only reach personal "perfection" in heaven, Paul says that the search for a fulfilled life (without egoism) is legitimate
1 Thessalonians 5,21: *"But test them all; hold on to what is good!"*

2/4 A philosopher, also fan of Friedrich Nietzsche, in an interview with us complained indignantly: "There are just as many genders and sexual orientations as people – this binary view of men and women is completely outdated!" What does "outdated" mean? And is the omnipresent, socially acceptable general condemnation of the Catholic Church not outdated?
REFUTATION:
Even if everyone "creates" their own sexual orientation, the generally acceptable definition of an "old-fashioned binary" division into male and female can be easily formulated: **It takes a *woman* and a *man* to claim our share in creation, namely, to conceive a child!** Genetic peculiarities or sexual needs of some people do not change that – God also loves such people and does not allow discrimination against them in the Bible. He calls for tolerance!

3/4 According to the impression of many people of our time, the differences between men and women should be "purposely destroyed through excessive philosophical debates". This, for example, is done by an internationally renowned female philosopher who – with all due respect – seemingly has a genderless appearance out of purpose and is a professor at a university in the USA. (Her name is known to us, but we will not disclose it here for reasons of fairness.)
REFUTATION:
We are convinced that tendencies to "argue away" the two sexes are deemed to fail, since **men and women are different.** Needs, characteristics, *similarities within both of the sexes* and also the *differences between* both of the sexes are very significant and can't just be taught or nurtured.
In contrast, Jesus and the Bible several times call for *equal rights* for both men and women!

4/4 A WithJesus-Employee knew a Doctor of Philosophy, head of a home for disabled people, who received complaints because the carers working there smoked excessively in the house, despite the smoking ban. The WithJesus-Staff appealed to this philosopher several times that he should enforce the smoking ban, but he legitimized smoking with incredibly long, philosophical arguments and even said that "it is necessary to have neither rules nor limits for successful human coexistence".

REFUTATION:

"No rules and limits?" Then remove all the traffic lights from the streets and watch how the traffic chaos turns into traffic madness.

People *need* rules and limits to coexist!

Exactly these old Christian values which some philosophers talk to death (see refutations from point 1/4), *existentially enable* **any philosopher to diss-ect these values with many words in the first place:**

Do you believe that we would have a lot of time to philosophize about how many genders there are, if we all still lived in stilt houses and had to hunt the deer in order to survive? Then solidarity would be needed again in the extended family. We can find the concepts of family and reason instead of a culture of vengeance, forgiveness, charity, etc. regarding the misery of this world in – let's be honest – rather in so-called "Christian countries": A significantly better qua-lity of life, longer periods of peace, more equality for men and women and for different cultures, less crime or corruption can be found there. This does not mean that the so-called "Christian" countries have no "skeleton in the cup-board", meaning that they do have problems of their own. Wannabe-Christians (who were not real Christians) have committed crimes. But with all due respect: What would happen if you were to philosophize aloud about how many genders and sexual orientations there are in certain other countries? So, what should then be so "catastrophic" about (real!) Christians?

A recommendation of **David Hume**, a Scottish philosopher (1711-1776), sounds refreshingly logical for Christians and conforms with the Bible: Namely, to "closely explore one's own perceptions, the things that people see and feel, instead of being too quick to assume that things seemingly are the way people think they are at first sight."[23] (This also leads astrology ad absurdum)

In contrast, **Friedrich Nietzsche**'s (1844-1900) **nihilism** is inadequate for Christians. Here are a few statements: "... no absolute truths and values ... This results in a belief of absolute worthlessness that is meaninglessness." Nietzsche replaces God with the "thought of eternal return ... that all happenings have happened indefinitely often and will return indefinitely often". This contrasts

23 Hume, David: "Treatise on Human Nature". See 1.4.2.

88

with David Hume's view, mentioned above.
REFUTATION of Friedrich Nietzsche: see from page 13 of this book.

According to Nietzsche, the human who through "revaluing all values creates new values" is "superman, at the same time antichrist and overcomer of God... conqueror of nothing. The action of the new human being follows the driving force of the will for power...". Overcomer of God?
In history we see what godless people cause: War, slavery, destruction. Even if some of these people called themselves Christians: *These were not Christians!*
Real Christians follow Jesus' calls: Compassion, forgiveness, etc.
With all due respect: The fact that Nietzsche at the age of only 45 years, accompanied by delusions, fell into mental derangement only serves expectations.

Christians, in fact, do believe in absolute values, which are conveyed by life and the Bible: Love, gratitude, mercy and the prophecies of the Bible, which provide us with evidence for the existence of the supernatural with astonishing precision. We don't need to "conquer nothing" because there already "is" enough. Also nothing will recur indefinitely because ...
1/2 ... David Hume, mentioned above, already refutes this with his formulation of the induction problem.
2/2 ... creation has a beginning and at the end Jesus will come (see from chap. 2.0 and 6.0) – then something completely new will emerge.

We strongly advise against becoming an Antichrist, because this guy will be thrown into hell at the end and then, at the very latest, knows for sure what "the good" is – and will long for it in vain.

And who should be able to "overcome God", please? And let's be honest:
How could philosophies like Nietzsche help lonely or sick people or a starving orphan? What *helps* is to entitle God to help through *prayer and deed!*
Or put more simply, even if some philosophers might roll their eyes now: Do good things.
Whoever wants to be a Christian is obliged to active compassion.
Paul explains that some knowledge only costs time for living and distracts from the goal, in
1 Corinthians 8,1: *"... But knowledge puffs up **while love builds up.**"*

And this passage in the Bible is the reason for this chapter: Paul's clear **warning against false teachings** in
Colossians 2,8: *"See to it that **no one takes you captive** through hollow and deceptive philosophy, which depends on human tradition and the elemental spiritual forces of this world rather than on Christ."*

If you go *against* the tide of philosophy, esotericism and occultism, you get to the freshest water: *the true spring, Jesus.*

1/3 Only the Bible proves its supernatural origin and guarantees the greatest blessings, free for your life, from *the one loving & living God* of this universe. Proof: see Chapter 2.2ff.

2/3 Nobody needs exotic, mysterious or even stupid rituals, in order to receive God's blessings, His healing, His salvation, His solution to problems, such as loneliness and much more.
We only need to believe in Jesus, we are *now* allowed to go to His Father and to come to him as we are – like little children come to their loving parents!
God hears you, He wants to help you, see chap. 2.3 of this book.

3/3 The Bible and this book have innumerable tips: **The biblical path with Jesus is not a virtual world from Hollywood, not an instruction from an esoteric group, but an *even larger and, above all, real adventure* – and *you,* dear readers, play the main role** and even receive the required skills free of charge – see chapter 6.3 of this book.
This is what *Jesus* wants to say to *you personally,* dear readers:

Luke 19,10: *"... For the Son of Man came to seek and to save the lost."*

Luke 4,18: *"The Spirit of the Lord is on me, because he has anointed me to proclaim **good news** to the poor. He has sent me to **proclaim freedom** for the prisoners and **recovery of sight** for the blind, to **set** the oppressed **free,** to proclaim the year of the Lord's favor."*

Jesus will and wants to help you!
You can find out how, in the Bible and in this book.

4.0 But What About the Other Religions?

First of all: This chapter is not a "competition" between religions.
We urge you to please read this foreword first. At the end of this chapter there will be a summary with a conclusion.

Real **Christians respect other beliefs, help and pray for** *all* **people of** *all* **cultures and** *all* **religions.**

The purpose of this chapter is to **communicate, to clear up misunderstandings** and to attempt to create **new levels of discussion.**
We are describing other religions from the perspective of Christianity here.

Here, at this point, we won't call religions or their founders by name. This is *not* **about dragging something or someone "into through the dirt", rather we want to explain why Christians are so convinced of Christianity in this chapter.**

And why (one should never generalize) *at least most* Christians respect other religions, but don't believe their contents.

A first impression: Many non-believers seem to like using Christianity as a projection surface for criticism ...
• ... in a way that is often disproportionately emotional,
• with – sorry – accusations & rumours often unchecked,
• which *mostly have nothing to do* with Christianity or the content of the Bible,
• while in the case of other faiths which define themselves in relation to everything that is different through intolerance, sometimes silence prevails or worries are only expressed behind closed doors,
• or "exotic" beliefs are declared "good" unconditionally.

A second impression: Maybe Christianity is also so eagerly criticized because vengeance and violence are prohibited for real Christians because of Jesus' instructions? Criticizing Christianity is therefore quite safe ...
A popular point of critique for Christians is the "claim to exclusivity"
(please turn the page):

"Why should Christianity be the 'only true way to God'?"
"Why do Christians claim 'exclusivity for salvation' for themselves?"

What heats the minds of many non-Christians are, among other things, Bible passages such as these:
John 14,6 (this is what Jesus says personally): *"I am the way and the truth and the life. No one comes to the Father except through me!"*
Does that mean that you can only get into heaven and receive eternal life as a Christian and that all people of all other religions go to hell?
Nonsense that wouldn't be biblical. See chap. 6.3.

4.1 What does the astronaut Ulf Merbold have to do with this chapter? An amazing example!

The WithJesus-Team found a fascinating story for you:
When the "European Space Administration"[24] made an invitation to join the flight in the space shuttle at the end of the 1970s, only 12 of hundreds of candidates for astronaut training were left after a tough selection process. These 12 decided to make a game: Each one of them should hand in a piece of paper with the names of three candidates which they intuitively believed to be the most capable and therefore to be the first candidates for the flight in space. The majority voted for astronaut Ulf Merbold and two others, Merbold actually became the first German astronaut in the Space Shuttle. The hunch all of the men had came true![25]
The WithJesus-Team is convinced that the different religions developed similarly in this way: They are sets of rules which intuitively originated during the search for God. And so, a lot of people are right with their hunch, *feeling* **that ... God is alive.**

Christianity is neither a religion nor a set of rules, it is practiced compassion, forgiveness and the reconnection of people with God through His Son Jesus, who gives us eternal life and more offers.
Yes, it works. No, we didn't do drugs. :-)
And only in the Bible do we find evidence of supernatural inspiration the trace of a living God – see Chapter 2.2 from p. 13.

---

24 "ESA", European counterpart to the American space agency "NASA"
25 Merbold, Ulf: "Flight into space", Bastei / Lübbe, Bergisch-Gladbach, p.179

Conclusion: God revealed himself to people through the Bible, the Bible was written by Jews for the good of *all* people – and God dictated everything. Christians are *obliged* to respect other faiths too, because no Christian can by his own strength convince fellow human beings about Jesus, not even with the most carefully picked arguments – this can only be done by God through His Holy Spirit declares God through the prophe **Zechariah chapter 4, verse 6:** *"Not by might nor by power, but by my Spirit', says the Lord Almighty!"*

4.2 Other Religions from the Perspective of the Bible — What Christians do NOT Believe

Christians do not believe in reincarnation, also known as "transmigration of souls". Re-in-carnation means (lat.) "embodied in flesh again". This "spiritual concept" of two world religions states that someone can after death return in another body – in some spectra of these religions this can also possible in the body of an animal (sacred cows are something else).

Caution 1/2: reincarnation was never written in the Bible and was never "deleted" there.
That is a – sorry – baseless assertion that we keep hearing in interviews with esotericists who – sorry – have replicated this unchecked from others esotericists without being able to prove it or looking for enough background information on the matter.
The concept of the Bible is incompatible with that of reincarnation, because, among other things, many of the faiths with reincarnation neither contain a god nor a paradise, which the Bible with its verifiable prophecies confirms, see chap. 2.2 from p. 13.

The most popular Bible passage into which reincarnation is interpreted: in **Malachi 4:5** (last prophet of the Old Testament) "Elijah" is announced, an Old Testament prophet: *"See, I will send the prophet Elijah to you before that great and dreadful day of the Lord comes."* Jesus personally quotes this passage in Matthew, chapter 11 verse 13-15 about 470 years later. This, however, does not mean that Elijah is coming back into the world in another body (wouldn't he then also have a different name? :-)), but that somebody will come in a function similar to Elijah, which ultimately happened through John the Baptist. You can imagine it similar to a new super guitarist of African American descent who – with all due respect – is called "the new Jimi Hendrix" by the media.

Also, the assertion that "reincarnation is 'true', because the life experience of a human being would be lost" is at best theory. Because then the life experience of their incarnation of reincarnated people would still need to exist, something which has never been proven (except for rumours and Hollywood films). Every human being has the opportunity, even without reincarnation, to pass on their life experience to fellow human beings or their children. Sorry: Reincarnation has never been scientifically proven. **And there *never* was anything written about reincarnation in the Bible to this day.**

Achtung 2/2: Reincarnation is not to be confused with the "Rebirth in Jesus" (= "real" baptism) – Here's the Difference:
The "new birth in Jesus" has nothing to do with being born in a different body after one's death. "Born again in Jesus" means that you become a Christian, it's a kind of reset button = restart in life.

This relates to the following statement by Jesus in
John 3,3f: *"Jesus replied, "Very truly I tell you, no one can see the kingdom of God unless they are **born again!**"*
The disciples were shocked and then asked Jesus the following:
"How can someone be born when they are old?" Nicodemus asked. "Surely they cannot enter a second time into their mother's womb to be born?"
Thereupon Jesus explains baptism = rebirth in Jesus in
John 3,5: *"Very truly I tell you, no one can enter the kingdom of God unless they are born of **water** and the **Spirit**."**

What does that mean: *"Born of water and the Spirit"*?

• Here *"water"* means the **real, biblical baptism, *"baptizein"* in Greek = "to submerge".** "Pouring over" or "splashing" with water is – sorry – not biblical. **Childrens' baptism can't be in Jesus' will,** because a child cannot consciously decide for Jesus, something it should be able to do it for baptism.
• Here *"Spirit"* **means the *Holy Spirit,* which God gives at baptism and with** whose help we understand the Bible and that Jesus is God's Son:
The baptized person is a new person: born again in Jesus.
• With the external act of baptism, a person consciously presents – as a testimony to others – death by ***drowning their old self.***

94

- And with the rising out of the *water* the *resurrection of* their new self! Because *water* is often a metaphor for the Holy Spirit in the Bible.

A baptized person is born again: The new Pia, the new Janis – from the baptism onwards, God begins to make the baptized into their "originals", just as He originally planned. Free from past influences and hurts of life, one of which the true personality and individuality of many people can be distorted (see also chapter 6.3, step 3/7).
The Holy Spirit will begin to inspire us after we are baptized, giving us ideas and the right words as well as helping with decisions – **from now on we belong to God, to his kingdom, are newly born of** *water and the Spirit* **and God starts to repair our lives, bringing them to full bloom and to fulfilment. We are as if we were born again:**
Rebirth in Jesus = baptism with water and the Spirit = new start in life.

Christians don't believe in every prophet – for the Last Days the Bible announces many false prophets.
An esotericist told us enthusiastically that he met a man in India who is said to be a prophet and wanted to be "the reincarnation of Jesus" – for real! This man, quite well known in esoteric circles, wanted have demonstrated his supernatural abilities by "getting" a strange powder "out of the air" and distributing it free of charge to those around him. Upon closer inspection, this powder smells, looks, and feels like ... grated soap flakes. It is also like that. Furthermore – sorry – no one could tell us a prophecy of him or anything like what Jesus did, such as healings, when we asked. We bless this man and his friends.

Christians cannot believe an alleged prophet who wrote a book with the help of others due to his lack of reading and writing skills, in which there is *not a single* prophecy of *his own,* but only one about the Last Days copied from the Bible repeated several times. When asked about that the prophet wanted his book to be understood as prophecy alone. Another popular self-proclaimed prophet became world famous with a book full of alleged prophecies world famous – but none of them contain any details on time, place or persons, only metaphorical statements in which something can be interpreted into retrospectively. Furthermore, it contains astrological claims that are extremely flawed, and that even contemporary "professional" astrologers make fun of (God warns against astrology in the Bible! see chap. 3.1).
Christians do not need to believe the facts mentioned above. Because they

have the Bible, which proves its unique sovereignty with its announcements (precise = binding information on time, places and names) that have come true.

Christians can show that the Bible has not been corrupted, even if that is said over and over again. For example, an alleged prophet claims in his book that "no one can change the words of [his] God" (note: he didn't mean the God of the Bible!), but in a different passage claims that "God gave the Bible to the Jews and Christians, but they have falsified the Bible", but does not say what and where something would have needed to be written. A hotly debated topic on the Internet – "contradiction", "implausible", many of the reactions are like this.

Only someone who shows an unchanged "original Bible", proving that this is the older original, can ultimately prove the "falsification" of the Bible. Until now nobody has been able to do that. Conspiracy theorists claim that such an "original Bible" is in the catacombs of the Vatican, right next to X-files about crashed UFOs in Area 51, a few dusty Madonna reports about the end of the world and truth about the moon landing ... nonsense, of course not, end of irony!

Evidence of the unchangeability of the Bible in Chapter 2.7

Christians do not believe in spiritual attitudes that discriminate against even oppress women:
Ironically, a famous founder of a "gentle reincarnation religion" according to the opinion of many people supposedly once said: "One should beware of women. For every smart one there are a thousand stupid or bad. The character of a woman is more hidden than the paths the fish takes in the water. She is wild as a robber and just as devious. Rarely does she speak the truth: For her truth and lie are the same thing", further: "... so that the continuation of the [name of this religion] teaching will be reduced by 500 years, women should be allowed to found an order."

In another religion, according to tradition, an alleged prophet said: "It is allowed to have sexual intercourse with captured women ... if she was married, her marriage is annulled." "... Hell is created for fools: Women are the stupidest of fools" because they "are ungrateful", "lack intelligence and religious commitment" and can "lead men astray". A leading politician of this religion publicly in 2016 said: "Women must be put under total control", everything else is a "crime against [this religion]".

Christians believe in the Bible's instruction that men & women are equal.
Ephesians 5,21f: *"Submit to one **another** [note: men and women!] out of reverence for Christ. Wives, submit yourselves to your own husbands as you do to the Lord. [...] Husbands, love your wives, just as Christ loved the church [...]."*
And how did Jesus love the church? Selfless to the point of death – this is how, according to Jesus, married couples should love one another.

Christians do not believe in every prophet – especially not when they call for absolute intolerance towards those of different faiths.
An alleged prophet urged his believers: "Cut off the heads of those of different faiths, wherever (!) you find them ... and the ends of their fingers because they resisted [the god of this religion and his alleged prophet]!" "Do not make friends with people of other faiths*, especially not with Jews and Christians" or "... my riches will come from the shadow of my sword ... and whoever contradicts me will be humiliated and persecuted!" ***How should integration work like this?***
These statements were said several centuries after Jesus' invitation to "love your enemies, bless those, who hate you". Why?
A top politician, believer in this other religion, known for his denial of the holocaust, publicly said: "... buy yourself a rifle ... rifles silence the enemies [of our religion]! We don't know any absolute values other than total submission to the will [of the god of this religion]. The Christians and Jews say: You should not kill! But we say that killing equals the importance of a prayer when it is needed. Deception, deceit, conspiracy, fraud, stealing and killing are nothing but a means for the cause [of the God of this religion]!"

Another trigger for the most emotional discussions: The alleged prophet of this religion claims a country (whose capital is in its according to their scripture is not mentioned at all), which was already promised to another culture 2,000 years earlier for the blessing of all people. In his book he tells of an alleged "mysterious journey" to a spiritual building located in the said capital – but his followers only built this building more than 70 years *after* the death of the alleged prophet in the claimed country in order subsequently to construct a reference to it! Which building could the alleged prophet have meant in his book? His own historian (!) says that the building, that the alleged prophet describes is located about 1,000 kilometres outside the claimed land!
That is why Christians only believe in the Bible.
Christians are also foreign to all aspects of martial arts or war.

Worrisome: The major world religions (not Christianity!) are announcing a holy war with which they ultimately destroy all other cultures. The Bible tells that at the Last Days the nations will attack Jerusalem, the centre of Christianity. **The Christian bonus for all other cultures:** Then Jesus will come with a heavenly army to push back the attackers,
and Jesus & Jerusalem will be a blessing for *all* people of *all* nations!

The term religion means "observance of regulations".
Christianity is not a religion – Christianity is practiced love.

Christianity = the orders of Jesus to be non-violent and love are the only really peaceful or gentle solution to all problems in this world.
Because Jesus orders to all people unequivocally in
Luke 6,27: *"Love your enemies, do good to those who hate you, bless those who curse you, pray for those who mistreat you!"*

The Jews had 613 laws in the Old Testament including the famous 10 Commandments that everyone should know ("You should not lie", "Do not kill", etc. ...)
Jesus personally **summarized these 613 laws and the 10 commandments into only 2 commandments together – the famous "double commandment of love" in**
Mark 12,29: *"The Lord our God, the Lord is one. Love the Lord your God with all your heart and with all your soul and with all your mind and with all your strength.' The second is this: 'Love your neighbour as yourself.' There is no commandment greater than these."*

Christians through their faith learn that Jesus is the Son of God and are already getting to know God personally and will live with Him forever. All the other people will see God and Jesus when Jesus returns. **Jesus offers eternal life to people of all cultures.** *Only through faith that Jesus is the Son of God – only Christianity offers this and can prove all of this. This is the only way that the spiral of hate, of vengeance, of the many conflicts in humanity can be broken.*

Only in this way, only through Jesus love can remain.

5.0 Jesus and the Same Old Misunderstandings: Crusades? Witch Hunts? Child Abuse? Why Does God Allow Disasters?

5.1 Jesus' Message: Love
What People Make of It: A Horror

The message of Jesus is clear: Selfless love, partly to the point of self-abandonment. Christians are obliged to love even enemies, Jesus says in
Luke 6,27: *"But to you who are listening I say:* **Love your enemies,** *do good to those who hate you, bless those who curse you, pray for those who mistreat you. If someone slaps you on one check, turn to them the other also. If someone takes your coat, do not withhold your shirt from them. Give to everyone who asks you, and if anyone takes what belongs to you, do not demand it back. Do to others as you would have them do to you. If you love those who love you, what credit is that to you? Even sinners love those who love them."*
Please keep reading these words of Jesus in your Bible.

But now atrocities were committed by alleged "Christians": child abuse, crusades, witch-hunts, forced evangelization. Atrocities were committed by people from "Christian" countries in their African, Asian, etc. colonies.
The question arises: **Were these truly real Christians?**

Is someone a Christian who does *not* keep Jesus' message of love?

If we want to form an opinion about religions, we have to read their "operating instructions" and not what people make of them!
We will now clarify these constantly identical allegations one after the other:

99

5.2 Crusades? Witch Hunts? Child Abuse?

Again and again, Christians hear the same allegations from others "... and the crusades?", but interviews and more detailed inquiries by the WithJesus-Team left the impression that they neither have any idea of the background nor find it worth it to deal objectively with the story.

Here is the historical chronology of the Crusades:
In 639 AD Jerusalem was conquered by Islamic Arabs. *Islamic* Arabs? Before the Islamic conquest the Arabian Peninsula was mainly Christian, Jewish and Pagan. Mohammed at around 620 called out a new Monotheism in polytheistic Mecca according to his ideas, the Meccans felt threatened, attacked him and Mohammed, including his entourage, had to flee from them to Medina on July 16, 622. That was the beginning of the Islamic calendar, also called "n.H." = "after Hidjra". There, Mohammed soon asserted to have gotten permission from Allah, to spread Islam through Jihad (Holy War)[26]: "Prepare yourselves, with as much as you are able to raise in war power and battle steeds, in order to use it to intimidate God's and your enemies. ... If you meet with a group of unbelievers* (note: Mohammed meant people of different faiths *) and a fight ensues, be steadfast ..." (Sura 8,45f). This is how Mecca was conquered and Arab and Jewish tribes destroyed – unless they converted to Islam.

During Muhammad's lifetime they for the first time attacked, albeit unsuccessfully, Muslims Israeli territory, called Palestine back then (explanation p. 25). From one year after Muhammad's death (632) the advance of the Arab troops was unstoppable: The Muslims benefited from rifts within the Eastern Roman Empire, from its exhaustion from battle against the Persians (Sassanids) and from the rivalry against the Western Roman Empire and from the consequences of the Justinian plague: Within several waves, it killed a quarter and up to half of the population in both empires, even in North Africa all the way to England from May 541 onwards!
So, there was a massive lack of tax revenue and soldiers, which enabled the Islamic conquest of Egypt in 639 and enabled the occupation of Jerusalem by the Umayyads in 638.
With the occupation of Jerusalem, Muhammad's "successor" began Middle East conflict that basically continues to this day. First Jews and Christians were

26 Ibn Ishaq, p. 280, in Gabriel, Mark, "Jesus and Mohammed", 1st edition 2006, p. 72ff

able to live their lives and practice their faith more freely than in the previous Eastern Roman occupation. Over the years the different Islamic occupiers (some of which also fought bitterly among themselves) put more and more pressure on Jews and Christians, discriminated them through the Islamic penalty tax for people of different faiths, forced Jews to wear symbols on clothes (similar to National Socialism). Also, Jews were not allowed to own horses etc.

THE TRIGGER FOR THE CRUSADES: aHaving been protected initially from the Islamic occupiers, the Church of the Holy Sepulcher and the Holy Sepulcher itself were sacked and later demolished by the Fatimid Caliph al-Hakim!
(By the way: a surprising number of experts are of the opinion that it is actually the hill of Gologotha and the real tomb of Jesus).

Pope Urban II in 1095 called for a "iustum bellum", a "just war". In several waves, crusaders retook Jerusalem, lost it again, because replenishment from Europe was hardly possible due to these distances.

From a military point of view, it was a "legitimate defensive war" because it was neither started by Jews nor by Christians. This has been proven by studies.

The crusaders weren't Christians because they didn't behave as Christians, certainly not as "awakened", that is, real Christians.
The Pope who ordered the Crusades should have known Jesus' message in the Bible – and **Jesus commands absolute non-violence.**

There never was a "holy war" done by Christians! People who do are not Christians! Jesus forbade that! (John 18, 10 & 11)

The people of Israel made many offers to Muslims to peacefully live in Israel. **Therefore ...**

... *real* **Christians pray that Jews, Christians and Muslims – in the order of their "arrival" in Israel – can find a lasting harmonic solution together in the Holy Land!**

More info chap. 6.3.

Witch Hunts

A dark chapter, not just for several churches, but for humanity.
Because: **nowhere in the Bible does it say that anyone should be tortured.**
But again and again people in this world attack minorities or people who are different. Only in the Old Testament are there death sentences for certain offenses and passages at the beginning of the OT in Exodus 22,17 and in Deuteronomy 13, which ordered the death sentence for sorcerers among the Israelites who led their fellow believers to worship other idols.

Any form of prescribed violence is a no-go for real Christians, but the above biblical passages should be seen in the context of that time: There was always war everywhere, the Israelites needed to stick together due to the permanent threat by neighbouring peoples – every weakness, every apostasy from their faith could strengthen the enemies of the Israelites.

But the witch hunts took place *after* Jesus, i.e. in the time of New Testament – to act even harder in the Middle Ages than in the time of Old Testament is not Christian, but unchristian madness!

The witch hunt allowed arbitrary persecution: Whoever wanted to get revenge on someone and had connections to authorities or had more money, filed charges of allegedly seen occult activities of the later actual victim. They had to prove their innocence, which is called "wrong evidence" – in contrast to today's usual "in dubio pro reo", which means in case of doubt *for* the accused. The tortures were brutal and what was even more perverse was that in some cases minutes were meticulously taken, even the desperate screams of the tormented were written down.

The evil in the witch hunt was the persecutors! *And these were no Christians,* even if they called themselves Christians – because a real Christian doesn't do that! Jesus commands love, even for enemies!

Child abuse

Please forgive our very direct choice of words:
Are Christians "child fu***rs" or "altar boy fu***rs"?
You can guess what is written here instead of the "***" and what is meant by it.

But it is precisely these expressions that we have heard all too often in recent years! Reports of abuse of minors arise particularly in Catholic institutions: Allegedly celibacy is to blame, those responsible could not control their sexual desire due to years of pent-up sexual dissatisfaction anymore and abused the children.

In fact, there are three points to this:

1/2 A celibate life is not required in the whole Bible!
Paul even *recommends* marriage:

Celibacy or the celibate (Latin "caelebs") means "living alone or unmarried" or "celibate" and most likely goes back to the Synod of Elvira in 306 AD. Not all Christian priests are required to live a celibate life: Priests of the Eastern dioceses are only required to do this during ordination; Protestants, Anglicans and Old Catholics are allowed to marry.

Only Paul *recommends* and *not obliges,* specifically in a Bible passage (1 Corinthians, chap. 7) to remain single for God, not any more than that. Otherwise Paul recommends being alone for *a time at most,* for personal retreat, for a temporary retreat with God, for fasting, for reflection and prayer. For Paul knew about the weakness of men, see

1 Corinthians 7,2-5: *"But since sexual immorality is occurring, **each man should have sexual relations with his own wife, and each woman with her own husband.** [...] Do not deprive each other except perhaps by mutual consent and **for a time,** so that you may devote yourselves to prayer. Then come together again so that Satan will not tempt you because of your lack of self-control."*

But hey, oh my goodness, what does it say here:

Matthew 8,14-15: *"When Jesus came into Peter's house, he saw **Peter's mother-in-law** lying in bed with a fever."*

Hey guys, the supposed "founder" of the Catholics, Peter, had a mother-in-law! That means he was – married! Scandal! (Joke :-))

2/3 Other passages in which the Bible recommends marriage:

Genesis 2,18: *"The Lord God said, "**It is not good for the man to be alone. I will make a helper suitable for him."***"* (Of course, that applies also for the woman – for her there is a man :-))

Ecclesiastes 4,10: *"If either one of them falls down, one can help the other up. But pity anyone who falls and has no one to help them up."*

103

3/3 Numerous studies show that celibacy does not influence paedophilic tendencies, but that people who are already paedophiles are more likely to do so be attracted to celibacy.

The Bible clearly commands protection for children! Please read 1 Corinthians 6,9: *"Neither fornicators, nor idolaters, nor adulterers, nor lecheries, nor boy molesters nor thieves nor the greedy nor drunkards nor slanderers nor swindlers will inherit the kingdom of God."*
Matthew 18,6: *„If anyone causes one of these little ones – those who believe in me – to stumble, it would be better for them to have a large millstone hung around their neck and to be drowned in the depths of the sea."*

The content of the Bible clearly forbids harming children and gives notice Child molester at worst consequences! Period!

Jesus-Nazis? Were "Christians Nazis too"? No!

Were Hitler and the Nazis Christians too? No – an inciting lie!
Again and again Christians are confronted with this lie, with which some want to drag Christianity through the dirt. Unfortunately, the WithJesus-Team often heard this untruth from young people, especially from one other religion – this created an impression that there was an agenda to incite people against Christians. **Even if the Nazis wrote "God with us" and abused the cross as a sign: They were never Christians because they did not act like Jesus!**
So-called **"right-wing Christians"**, who preferably live in Texas and the surrounding area, nurture racist thoughts and assert, among other things, that "all people of other faiths go to hell", which doesn't correspond at all with the Bible! Thus: Not Christians.
The true, radical Christian does not kill people, but saves lives, even risking his or her life! At this point only a few of thousands of Christians will be mentioned, who, despite the risk of being murdered by the Nazis, saved lives:
Bishop Clemens August Graf von Galen hindered National Socialist murders of disabled people. The later educated Catholic war profiteer, womanizer, but devout[27] Oskar Schindler remembered Christian values and saved the lives of over a thousand Jews, the **students of the "Weiße Rose"** (engl. = "White

---

27 Welt.de Online, Facius, Gernot, "Das späte Erbe des Retters", https://www.welt.de/print-welt/article587926/Das-spaete-Erbe-des-Retters.html, Oct. 18, 1999, retr. on March 27, 2018

Rose", resistance movement against Nazis) with leaflets called their fellow human beings to resist these atrocities and were beheaded.

Many pastors were imprisoned in Nazi concentration camps and also often brutally murdered due to their efforts to **help Jews** and protest against the persecution of Jews: **Paul Schneider,** the "Preacher of Buchenwald", **Dietrich Bonhoeffer** and many more. In the "priest block" of the Dachau concentration camp and others hundreds of religious sisters and friars were murdered just because they followed Jesus and not Hitler. Do you know **Corrie ten Boom**? This heroine of Christianity in a secret room behind her bedroom rescued the lives of many Jews in the occupied Netherlands, was betrayed, imprisoned, but survived the torture in the concentration camp – her sister, however, was killed.

5.3 "Why Does God Allow Disasters?" What Is Sin, What Is Hell?

With all due respect, an apt answer to the above question: If you are stuck at the side of the road with a flat tire and you don't call the breakdown service then this is neither the fault of the car manufacturer nor of the breakdown service if you have to wait for help. If you want to receive help, you should call as quickly as possible- the breakdown service is there for you.

Likewise, God is there for us, but far too many people *still don't let Him* **into their lives – by accepting the belief in Jesus as the Son of God which would restore their connection with God.** And this is exactly the number one cause why people come into need and live in a fallen creation in which there is sickness, misery, hatred, tragedy and much more (as beautiful as it can be here on earth).

How we can get maximum blessings, protection, and help from God (which God wants to give us anyway!), **is written in chapter 6.3.**

"Why didn't God prevent this or that bad thing?" many ask.

Answer: **Because we usually don't give God enough rights to help us! A gift from God to us is our** *free will* **– we can decide** *for* **or** *against* **God – He will respect it.**

Most of the bad that happens to us on earth is man-made.

But natural disasters or accidents for which no one is to blame leave behind victims. But even here God could protect more if we would let Him.

These are the reasons for tragedies that strike some of us:

1/3 Original Sin & sin: Eve was seduced by the serpent, to eat an apple from the tree of knowledge despite of God's ban to do so. Adam also let himself be seduced to do so. Both were then thrown out of paradise by God. We don't completely know how it went exactly, because the text can be seen more as a text of revelation, but the consequence of the matter is the fall of man: **We live here on earth** *separated from God* **– that is the original meaning of the word "sin" and *not* "something indecent or doing evil". Doing evil *causes* sin = separation from God. If we disregard the instructions of Jesus for our lives (obey 10 commandments, forgiveness, bless enemies, etc.), then we exclude God, His help, protection and blessings from our lives.**

2/3 Guilt and ancestral guilt / inherited sin: if, for example, a grandfather fraudulently takes possession of property, the grandchildren may not know about it, but benefit from what is stolen family-owned money – that deprives God of the right to bless the grandchildren!
This principle works even with whole nations! If, for example, Germany stole property from Jews in the Third Reich or from colonial countries such as England or France have exploited people in their colonies in order to finance their industry or social systems, for example, whole strata of the population benefit from this without even realizing it. And even if one day nobody from these times will be alive anymore the population of these countries will still bear the fault as a nation – because that's where this "bloody" money is seeping away. And which nation is completely guiltless?
Treason, fraud, infidelity, theft – whether one person or large groups.
But that also applies to spiritual or emotional offenses: Occultism, sexual violence, refused help, nationalism, national socialism, alcohol and drug addiction, pornography, greed, exaggerated thinking about security (= motion of no confidence in God!), All of this causes sin.
The following generations also bear the consequences of such fault: The curse of dishonestly earned profit will eventually turn into loss, quarrel, illness, misery, rift and in the worst case, war.
Long-term consequences of sin can be recognized in recurring patterns since generations, if for example some families "always had bad luck": Illnesses, depression, failed marriages, inability to form healthy relationships, unemployment, addiction problems with drugs, alcohol, money or power, existential problems etc. **OUT, off to freedom with Jesus! See chap. 6.3**

3/3 Job trial, "thorn in the flesh", sudden death: When we read Job's story in the Bible, we see that Job was tempted by the devil, but clung to God in spite of all trials. A Job-trial is rare, but **often, when Christians cling to God despite the most adverse circumstances, God gets more spiritual rights to help the people on this earth than through America's most successful TV pastors.**
Paul tells us about the "thorn in the flesh" in
2 Corinthians 12, 7: *"Therefore, in order to keep me from becoming conceited, I was given a **thorn in my flesh**, a messenger of Satan, to torment me."*
What, Paul, one of the greatest heralds of Jesus' love message, had a *"thorn in the flesh"*? Yes, for he was a man mightily anointed by God, but God knew that Paul would become arrogant in front of his fellow men and that he would "drift away" if Paul would not get a kind of "brake" in his life.

On a small scale, parents sometimes need to not allow the child to do something to protect them from harm and the child cries "snot and water" about its mean parents: No more chocolate, no more ice cream in the evening, and the 17-year-old girl need to be picked up from the club at 11pm by her dad – how embarrassing! :-)
This means:
On a large scale, God sometimes has to set limits in life for us. Then suddenly plans fail and we suffer setbacks. CEOs who become Christians have lost their jobs because of God-ordained changes in their lives. An arrogant professional guitarist, who just became a Christian, needs to put his guitar job on hold for two years for the sake of another job. God sometimes allows such changes to be made so that people can learn to focus their new life on Him, to develop a relationship and trust with him, to get their feet on the ground in order to not become arrogant. Because this happens a lot faster than you might think: When people succeed a lot, they quickly forget how God takes care of them and instead they believe they are able to do everything without God. Paul was aware of this!
The WithJesus-Team knows a young man who has had cancer for a long time, who says: "If I hadn't got the disease, I would be already dead because of my previous way of live – but then I wouldn't spend eternity with Jesus and my loved ones in paradise ..."

Sometimes innocent people or innocent children die and sometimes Christians suddenly, unexpectedly or tragically also do.
That is why we are often asked: "But what if even Christians are not protected,

what is the point of being a Christian?" Let's step into God's shoes: **What does God want? He wants to spend eternity with us in paradise (= heaven)**! But He already knows *beforehand* (in this way He could also give us the prophecies of the Bible) that some people would completely drift away from Him. So, God calls some people to Him prematurely before He is no longer able to reach them. Of course, He could impose His will on us and enable us to have the "perfect life", but then we would be puppets and not people who can freely choose Jesus.

Does Hell Exist?

Many people do not want to imagine that there is a hell in which some people will suffer for the rest of eternity. What does the bible say about that?
Old Testament: Daniel 12,2-3: *"Multitudes who sleep in the dust of the earth will awake: some to everlasting life, others to shame and **everlasting contempt.** Those who are wise will shine like the brightness of the heavens [...] for ever and ever."*
New Testament, Matthew 13,41: *"The Son of Man* [note: Jesus] *will send out his angels, and they will weed out of his kingdom everything that causes sin and all who do evil. They will throw them into the blazing furnace, where there will be weeping and gnashing of teeth."*
The Bible definitely says that unfortunately not all people go to heaven. **Anyone who turns to Jesus Christ *honestly* is forgiven of all sins, see chap. 6.3 of this book. Whoever could never get to know Jesus is judged according to their conscience and their attitude of heart**: A child or an indigenous person in the jungle eating human flesh, or child soldiers have, shall we say, they have their "own" idea of what is right and wrong and are not always aware that he / she are causing pain to other people. But people who consciously reject God or Jesus live in sin: Not because they steal, secretly masturbate. **But people who consciously reject God or Jesus live in sin:** Not because they steal, secretly masturbate, watch porn movies or earn a little tax-free side income, but because through their actions or their mindset *behind everything* they **cause separation from God** – THAT is the original meaning of the term "sin": To be *separated from God!*

In practice you can think of it as follows:
You meet someone dying of thirst in the desert and want to show them the way to a water source, but this person rejects it out of pride, mistrust, or a know-it-

all manner ... and dies of thirst. Is that your fault or that of the water source? No. Thus it is also not God's fault if people refuse God and His blessings, and therefore lead an unhappy life, after their death missing their access to eternal life in God's love. God respects the free will of these people and because of their heart's attitude gets no access to them. And so many people will be lost ... unfortunately! :-(

Theoretically, even a murderer who repents and recognizes Jesus as the Son of God his personal Saviour, can be redeemed and go to heaven. But some people who have done something wrong can only often cope by suppressing the fact that man is an eternally living creature and they, for example, have to expect seeing their victims again in the hereafter and thus also God. They suppress the factor of the supernatural and the fact of a living God, fail to repent and therefore cannot claim Jesus Christ's sacrifice on the cross and ... block their way to heaven. In one sentence:

It is not God who blocks people's access to heaven, but people themselves – basically a lot of people are building hell for themselves.

Hell is less of a place, more of a state: *Separated from God.*

In a prophetic dream a Christian from the WithJesus-Team probably stood in front of the gates of hell, *shortly before he decided (!) for Jesus.* "I stayed in a friend's new house and prayed for a dream that should show me what the future holds – many people know this 'tradition'. The next morning, I found myself trying to push away what I had dreamed of. I was shocked when I remembered the extraordinarily realistic dream: I was walking slowly on one long plank that went slightly downhill towards a gigantic wall of fire. But I didn't feel at risk, it was so comfortable ... downhill, towards the end of the plank closed ... until I suddenly realized how close my end was and turned back with the utmost force of my will, running back! I had no idea what made my subconscious dream this, I hadn't seen a horror movie before, nor read something about flames, hell or the like, nor had I even sat in front of a campfire. The only way I can explain this is that God had announced my imminent salvation back then!"

But now the good news: How we allow God as much as possible to help us to lead a maximally blessed, fulfilled and abundant life! See chapter 6.3!

5.4 The Bible, the "Operating Instructions for Christians" (©WithJesus) - Is it "Bloodstained", "Medieval" or "Misogynist"?

We often hear that the Bible is "medieval" and "discriminates against women" because it contains this one guy with the horns, his demons and also many wars. The well-known German management trainer, Vera Birkenbiehl, says that "the Bible is at least as cruel as the Koran".[28] Many believe that the Jews committed genocide of the locals when they conquered Israel: The complete annihilation of several tribes.

What is true? What do the facts say? Here clarification, one after the other:

I/3 "Bloodstained Bible?" - "Genocide ordered by God"?

Why did God order the Israelites to destroy some tribes during the capture of the promised land of Canaan (= Israel)? Why so cruel?
Here are two scriptures that explain this:
Deuteronomy 7,1: *"When the Lord, your God, brings you* [note: the Israelites] *into the land you are entering to possess and drives out before you many nations:* **the Hittites, Girgashites, Amorites, Canaanites, Perizzites, Hivites and Jebusites** *..."*

Deuteronomy 18,9: *"When you enter the land the Lord your God is giving you, do not learn to imitate the detestable ways of the nations there. Let no one be found among you who* **sacrifices their son or daughter in the fire,** *who practices divination or sorcery, interprets omens, engages in witchcraft, or casts spells, or who is a medium or a spiritist or who consults the dead. Anyone who does these things is detestable to the Lord; because of these same detestable practices the Lord your God will drive out those nations* [note: the nations mentioned above] *before you."*

Conclusion – albeit difficult to digest for Christians:
God ordered the Israelites to destroy these peoples who lived before them in Israel, not only because they were completely devoted to occultism, but *even burned their children as sacrifices to idols.*

---

28 YouTube.com, Birkenbiehl, Vera F, "Vera F Birkenbihl Vera F Birkenbihl What we need to know about the Islamic world", https://www.youtube.com/watch?v=a8N5g0Qxn1A, 28.5.2019, May 28, 2019, ab. at the December 4, 2020

Almost everyone knows the story of the desperate Abraham, who should sacrifice his own son Isaak[29] on "Mount Morija", today's Temple Mount, for God. Incredible! But, **1st:** The Israelites experienced or heard God much more immediate at that time and **2nd: The Bible testifies that the Israelites during their conquest of the promised land met peoples who sacrificed children to their idols** – that was apparently "common" back then – madness!

Even the Israelite king Ahaz allowed himself to be led into it and **(2 Kings 16,2f)** *"... and even sacrificed his son in the fire, engaging in detestable practices of the nations the Lord had driven out before the Israelites."*
The result: Through this atrocity, Ahaz shut himself and his people off from the blessing God's and a foreign occupying power came into the country.

Abraham probably thought: "Now God wants a child sacrifice from me too", **but God stopped Abraham with His angel before sacrificing Isaac to demonstrate that the God of the Bible *does not* want child sacrifice!**

From the above Bible passage, the reason is clear: These tribes should be destroyed because they sacrificed their children to their idols.
At the time the Israelites began to settle in Israel and afterwards were constantly led into battles and wars *everywhere*. That's why there was within the Israelites also the death penalty for "splitters": The people had to stick together under all circumstances, otherwise it would be instantly destroyed or enslaved by other peoples. That is why the Old Testament (the Bible up to the birth of Jesus) is not always easy to read for Christians either.

In *no part* of the Bible are the Israelites or Jews commanded to sacrifice children or to conquer *the whole world* by force.
DVDs and comics by the Turkish national religious department caused a scandal in Germany in 2016, because they should make martyrdom palatable for children of this other religion.[30]
What does God in the Bible say about child abuse? Please turn the page ...

---

29 This story is also mentioned in the Koran, but in a different way: Isaac's name is used in older ranen not mentioned, but in more recent Korans with Abraham's illegitimate son Ishmael (first as a footnote). According to the Bible, God's covenant exists with Isaac: Genesis 17,19
30 tagesspiegel.de online, "How nice to be a martyr!", http://www.tagesspiegel.de/kultur/comics/kontroverse-um-comic-wie-schoen-ein-maertyrer-zu-sein/14505862.html, 6.9.2016, down. on January 31, 2018

The God of the Bible wants the protection of children! Period!

Jeremiah 32,35: *"They built high places for Baal in the Valley of Ben Hinnom to sacrifice their sons and daughters to Molek, though I never commanded – nor did it enter my mind."*
That means, according to the Bible, applies to Jews and Christians:
Deuteronomy 5,17: *"You shall not kill!"*
Leviticus 19,18: *"... you shall love your neighbour as yourself."*
Matthew 18,3 (quote from Jesus): *"Truly I tell you, unless you change and become like little children, you will never enter the kingdom of heaven."*

2/3 Is the Bible "Medieval?"

No – the Bible is timelier than ever. Medieval? Read the newspaper or watch the news on TV then you will see exactly how barbaric and medieval mankind deals with each other today. And that peace in the "more civilized" countries of the world absolutely can't be taken for granted, only because of God's grace. **Let's be honest: the most peaceful and tolerant countries in the world rather are the Christian ones ...**

Yes, there are many references to the devil and demons in the Bible. But who are these nasty guys? The devil was once the angel Lucifer, the "light bringer". He revolted against God, whereupon God repudiated him – therefore he is also called "the fallen angel". **This is what the Bible says:**
Luke 10,18: *"He replied* [note: Jesus]*, 'I saw Satan fall like lightning from heaven ...'"*
Revelation 12,3: *"The great dragon was hurled down- that ancient serpent called the devil, or Satan, who leads the whole world astray. He was hurled to the earth, and his angels with him."*
The former chief angel Lucifer was not satisfied with his post and wanted to be equal to God. He rejected Lucifer and all of the angels of his gang fell with him. These fallen angels are the demons who confuse people and give them crazy ideas. The demons are given the right to influence *those* people who act contrary to the love message of Jesus and do evil.

But is that medieval? No Because: **Demons or "evil spirits" are the most "interreligious" thing in human history:** No matter whether in the big monotheistic religions, in Islam, in Buddhism, in Hinduism, in Natural religions with one or more gods – strangely enough *all* religions of the world speak of "good and bad spirits".

Is the existence of angels and demons so absurd? Please imagine, there would be other physical laws in this world, and we could only fly around through thoughts and be angels. Ultimately, we also only move our limbs through the "power of thought": "Physics of will" someone once said. And then one of your angel neighbours would whisper to you, "supposedly there are people, and they are unable to fly ..." Would you believe it then? There are credible reports of children after near-death experiences who completely astonished asked their parents after they've awakened: "I've seen angels – but they don't have any wings!" They don't need them – their flight does not depend on air.

The Bible tells incredible things in the Gospels and in Acts: That Jesus often freed people afflicted by demons who couldn't have known anything at all about Jesus, even less that this was the Son of the Living God and the demons addressed Jesus as the Son of God *directly* through the afflicted person. A creepy situation that we can really imagine is how possessed people are portrayed in some Hollywood horror movies: There stands a young, pretty girl with rolled eyes and says creepy things in the voice of a really bad beer drinker and smoker ... Brrr!

Ephesians 6,12: *"For our struggle is not against flesh and blood, but against the rulers, against the authorities, against the powers of this dark world and against the spiritual forces of evil in the heavenly realms."*
That is, Christians should not condemn evil people, but rather the *evil behind it,* that seduces people and incites them to war, quarrels, revenge, and other lower needs.

And if we as Christians think this Bible passage through, then we shouldn't participate in the madness of our time but should motivate each other to follow the instructions of Jesus through loving our enemies, showing mercy and practicing forgiveness as role models. (siehe Matthew 5,44)

And this call to love from the Bible is not medieval, because this world needs nothing *more necessary* than love – *to turn this need* in humanity towards love and peace.
Turn your faith to knowledge: When you will become a Christian and ask God, he will surely let you hear His voice. Or let you see an angel.

Many Christians have seen angels! Do you want that too? It works!
One of the authors of this book was able to experience that twice – no, we don't take drugs. Here is his report: "I went to a wedding of born-again Christians, the church building was very full, all guests were overjoyed, it was a joyful celebration! I sat down with friends, we had a lot of fun – but when the wedding and the church band started playing, the Holy Spirit touched me and I almost began to cry with emotion – suddenly I saw the roof of the community building "open" and also saw, similar to baroque paintings, a radiant sky above me, extending for miles with a vertical tunnel of clouds between which myriads of angels flew and sung songs of praise, because two more Christians had found one another in love again! I hadn't had any alcohol on this night!" Dear readers, you can experience something like this too!

And there are even bigger miracles right before your eyes: Imagine that space was completely empty. Because it would actually make more sense, if *nothing* existed at all!
Suppose you could fly around unnoticed in this completely empty space, and you suddenly discover a stone that is floating there (yes that is illogical, it's just an example). You would then ask yourself where this stone came from even though nothing exists at all. Because the whole space should actually be empty! From a logical viewpoint a "final" question would be why *anything* exists *at all!* We can be all the more surprised and happy that not just one stone exists but that suns, at least a planet with life, with people who are able to be creative exist – *that* is the real miracle!

There is Aaron's staff (Numbers 17,23), **that starts blooming overnight or a lady who get pregnant by the Holy Spirit** (Mary), **the easiest tasks for God! Jesus says to God, His Father:** *"... everything is possible for you."* (Mark 14,36)

3/3 Is the Bible "Misogynistic"?

No, that is nonsense. Men and women are equal in the Bible:
Ephesians 5,21: *"Submit to one another out of reverence for Christ! Wives, submit yourselves to your own husbands as you do to the Lord. For the husband is the head of the wife as Christ is the head of the church, his body, of which he is the Saviour. Now as the church submits to Christ, so also wives should submit to their husbands in everything.* **Husbands, love your wives, just as Christ loved the church."**

"... women submitting to their husbands ..." **We already hear quite a few women sigh at this,** but please take note of the next sentence:

"Husbands, love your wives, just as Christ loved the church."
And how did Jesus love the church? Selfless until death!
This is how **Christian men should love their wives ...**

Both husband and wife should *mutually* submit and *mutually* serve another. Some also interpret this passage as follows: The man is the head of the woman, because if one day the woman has a baby, she must completely focus on the little one. It's up to the man to take responsibility for decisions which were decided together to protect his wife and their baby.

The term head is also not intended here as the superior position of the man, but as the "origin", since women were taken from the rib of a man. Jewish rabbis like to explain this passage as follows: The woman was not taken from the man's head so that she doesn't rule over him, not from his feet, so that she might serve him, but from the rib, because this is closest to the heart! If that's not romantic ...

An often critically mentioned passage from the Bible is this in
1 Corinthians 14,34: *"Women should remain silent in the churches. They are not allowed to speak, but must be in submission, as the law says."*

Here is the most likely historical background: the pagan niche traditions were actually detrimental to women.
Then Jesus came and ordered equality between men and women.
At that time, people still needed to take small "development steps" to get used to the new times. In order not to cause chaos in the service, this was a provisional measure.

And: of course, the men in Corinth also had to be subordinate in the order of their community.

Paul also sees women as equal in his other letters – not only that, but he also challenges women to learn and men to take on great responsibility:
1 Corinthians 14,35: *"If they want to inquire something, they should ask their own husbands at home ..."*

115

People – not matter if they are men or women – who would have discovered their freedom "overnight", wouldn't have been "mature" enough for an orderly discussion in the church community. Therefore, women should also ask men their questions at home – **which brings men into pastoral responsibility,** to be loving and competent mediators of the good news for their wives.

There are many women in the Bible who have had leadership responsibilities: the **judge Deborah** in Judges 4:4-9. The **prophetess Hulda** in 2 Kings 22,14. The **prophetess Miriam** in Exodus 15:20.
Micah 6,4: *"I brought you up out of Egypt and redeemed you from the land of slavery. I sent Moses to **lead you,** also Aaron **and Miriam."***

In the Old Testament there is a characteristic passage for this topic in
Genesis 3,16: *"... and he will [!] rule over you."*
This passage must also be viewed in the context of the original Hebrew text, because here the word "should" isn't written. So, this point is not an order given by God, that the man should rule over the woman, *but (once again) a prophecy come true* that the man *will* later rule over the woman. But that did not come from the culture of the Jewish people, but from the later **Greek way of life which often created disadvantages for women.**[31]

Here is a note on the equality of God Himself from the
Genesis 1,26: *"Then God said, 'Let us make mankind in our image, in our likeness, so that they may rule over ... all the creatures that move along the ground.'"*
God has created *man **and** woman* in his image and *both* of them shall rule the earth.
1 Peter 3,7: *"Husbands, in the same way **be considerate as you live with your wives,** and treat them with respect as the weaker partner ..."*
In Acts 2, *man **and** woman* receive the Holy Spirit.

Jesus also defended women! Here are two small examples:

In John 4, verse 6 Jesus is sitting at a well in the midday heat, when a Samaritan woman wants to draw water there. At that time, Samaritans were seen as inferior. Even so, Jesus politely asks them to give him a drink – he didn't have a vessel with him! And Jesus reveals himself to her as the Son of God, the Christ, in the parable with the living water. Please read this beautiful story in your Bible!

31 Recommended literature: Iwersen, Julia, "The Woman in Ancient Greece", 2002

In John 4, verse 6 the arrogant Pharisees bring an adulteress caught in the act to Jesus and remind Him that following the law of Moses she must be stoned – but Jesus counters with astonishing quick-wittedness:
"Whoever of you is without sin, let him throw the first stone!"
The Pharisees knew that each of them had committed sins, whereupon they couldn't think of anything better than … to leave wordlessly …
Jesus saved that woman's life.

Important question: To whom do you believe the risen Jesus first shows himself after his horrific death on the cross? To the women!

Matthew 28,1ff: *"After the Sabbath, at dawn on the first day of the week,* **Mary Magdalene** *and the* **other Mary** *went to look at the tomb. […] An angel of the Lord came down from heaven and, going on the tomb, rolled back the stone and sat on it. […] The angel said to the women, 'Do not be afraid, for I know that you are looking for Jesus, who was crucified. […]* **Suddenly Jesus met them.** *'Greetings', he said. […] 'Do not be afraid.* **Go and tell my brothers to go to Galilee.'"**
Jesus not only gives his first encounter after the resurrection Women, but **Jesus trusts women to transmit the incomprehensible message of the resurrection – this is how Jesus entrusted women!**
Summary from the perspective of the Bible and Christians:

1/3 man and woman are different, but that is exactly what makes it possible for them to truly complement each other in marriage.
2/3 man and woman are clearly equal for Jesus.
3/3 **Both** are the image of God, both are to rule over the earth (of course responsibly), both should represent God on earth and are authorized to do so!

Galatians 3,28: *"… nor is there male and female, for you are all* **one** *in Christ Jesus."*

1 Corinthians 11,12: *"For as woman came from man, so also man is born of woman.* **But everything comes from God."**

More information on equality between men and women on page 87.

6.0 How You Can Benefit from Jesus – Here We Go!

6.1 Who Is Jesus? Who Is Christ?
And Who Is the Holy Spirit?

Jesus was a Jew, learned the trade of carpenter, never had sex or a wife. Yes, that is possible, members of the WithJesus-Team also have lived celibacy for a time in order to reflect on God. If you honestly intend to do so, then God gives you the ability to fast: from chocolate, alcohol, the screen and much more. But, not that you can "suffer artificially", but so that you can empty yourself in order for God to fill = enrich = bless you with wisdom, new talents, insights, inspiration, new perspectives and much more.

No, Jesus was "never in India where He learned all the tricks" – that's something we often hear from many esotericists and it is – sorry – unchecked nonsense, repeated without questioning or proving it.

Von Jesus zu profitieren ist so einfach, dass viele Menschen es kaum glauben können. Or want to believe it? Many people seem to find it easier to gain or painfully achieve a "higher spiritual level" through tiring meditation, fasting as self-punishment, absurd rituals and dances, sitting positions which damage the meniscus and much more. Out of pride?

In Christianity this is not necessary: Everything is given to you.

You are a Christian if you believe that ...

1/3   ... Jesus Christ is the Son of God and ...
2/3   ... Jesus volunteered himself on the cross to "pay" for the sins of *all*
       Had people murdered (including *you,* dear readers!) ...
3/3   ... whereby all people who believe in point 1/3 and 2/3 and "follow"
       Jesus = obey, love & forgive 10 commandments,
       therefore they are blameless before God = without sin,
       thus, come back into personal contact with God,
       whereby God is allowed in to be in their lives,
       to help them live full and abundant lives
       and afterwards gifts them eternal life in paradise with Him. Finished.

Yes, that sounds a bit stupid to "outsiders". Even for us before we became Christians. But it works! **The 3 points systematically explained:**

1/3 Jesus is the Son of God, that is what Jesus himself says in **John 14,6:** *"I am the way and the truth and the life. No one comes to the Father except through me!"* For proof see chap. 2.2ff.
There are religions that say, "Jesus cannot be the Son of God because for that God would have needed a wife!" Christians, however, believe in an *omnipotent* God who does not need a woman to create about people.
All true Christians are God's children – but Jesus was God's very special child.
Now who is the Holy Spirit? It is God *in His function as a Holy Spirit.* Jesus announces Him to Christians in
*John 14,16: *"And I will ask the Father, and he will give you another advocate to help you and be with you* ***forever*** *–* ***the Spirit of truth.*** *The world cannot accept him because it neither sees him nor knows him. But you know him, for he lives with you and will be in you."*
This was also announced by the prophet about 835 years *before* Jesus
Joel 3,1-2: *"And afterward, I* [note: God] *will pour out my Spirit on all people. Your sons and daughters will prophesy, your old men will dream dreams, your young men will see visions. Even on my servants, both men and women, I will pour out my Spirit those days."*

Important: nobody can believe in Jesus "by themselves" (see points 1/3 & 2/3). You can only believe that Jesus is God's Son if God when God gives you this faith through His Holy Spirit and you accept this faith. If that's what you want (hopefully): *please please* **ask God** *now,* **in your words, that He gives makes the good news of Jesus and the content of the Bible understandable for you.** Yes, that sounds stupid, but please, trust us, give it a try. If you are sitting on the train, a prayer in your mind also counts if it's sincere. Something like this: "Please, God, in the name of Jesus, open my heart and mind with your Holy Spirit so that I may learn to understand Your living word in the Bible!"
It actually works! If not now, then soon. Do not give up! Here Jesus *personally* asks His disciples who they think He is:
Matthew 16,13-20: *"'But what about you?' he asked. 'Who do you say I am?' Simon Peter answered, 'You are the Messiah, the Son of the living God.' Jesus replied, 'Blessed are you, Simon son of Jonah, for this was not* ***revealed to you by***

119

flesh and blood, but by my Father in heaven!'"
John 6,44 (quote from Jesus): *"No one can come to me unless* **the Father** *who sent me* **draws them.** *"*

2/3 "But I'm not a sinner, I haven't done anything wrong! Why do I need Jesus then?" We also hear that often. Answer: so that you can …
… be free from "sin" and "original sin" – what is that anyway? The term "sin" is distorted due to an often-incorrect transmission of biblical content – in families, media, even schools. Most often think about things like a child who stole a banknote out of grandma's handbag stolen, a politician who is lets himself be seduced by bribes, a wife who betrays her husband, and (this book also wants to address taboo topics), a teenager who masturbates behind the secretly acquired porn magazine.
But that is *not* "sin", **it is the mindset** *behind* **certain acts** (theft, hatred, violence, lies, occultism, materialism etc. – not masturbating) **only causes sin:**

Sin is separation from God! When someone does want to invite God into their life or locks him out with the evil deeds mentioned above and blocks God's offer of blessings, help, protection & inspiration.

Sin is written in the Hebrew Old Testament as "chat'at" and referred to as "hamartia" in the New Testament, which is written in Greek. Both terms mean "missing [a target]". The word "sin" comes from Germanic laguages: Old English "synn", Old Norwegian "synd", which comes from the Indo-European "es", the participle of verb "to be" like "being" in the sense of "the one who it was".

Original sin is the first sin, namely that of Adam and Eve that caused the fall of man. Right, it's the story with the apple found quite at the beginning of your Bible: Adam and Eve lived happily in paradise with God but were not allowed to eat the fruits of the "tree of life". We remember that the snake offers Eve the apple. Eve eats it, though she knows that God does not want that, and also tempts Adam to do that. As a response, God throws them both out of paradise – the fall of man (Genesis, chapter 3)! **From this the principle or** *the essence of sin originated:* **Separation from God!**

We all who live here on earth carry this original sin ranging from the newborn baby to an elderly person, *all* **people of** *all* **countries of** *all* **cultures.**

Original sin = all people are separated from God.
Unless you become a Christian. Then your sin is erased by your faith, and you will come into personal contact with God again! (See chapter 2.3)

God created two areas in order to protect & support us:
1) an area of His will where there is blessing: Love, forgiveness (also for enemies!), mercy, living the 10 commandments – and believing in Jesus.
2) the area outside of His will where there is no blessing: Hatred, deceit, theft, selfishness, occultism, materialism – and rejecting Jesus.

We get the most blessings when we recognize and do God's will – does that mean I am not allowed to have a will of my own? Of course, you can!
Because the deepest and most sincere desires of the heart that people carry within themselves, are those that God has put in us! **You may have wishes:** **Psalm 37,4:** *"Rejoice in the Lord, and he will give you what your heart desires."*

But that doesn't mean that God fulfils selfish wishes – an example:
Stefan, 40, didn't get enough attention from his parents in his childhood and youth and was teased at school. Now he desperately wants to become a managing director of a technology company. Then he would finally have control over other people. He believes that this wish would make up for his suffering ... and suppresses the fact that he would in actuality rather have become a paediatrician, which God put on his heart and planned with him – Stefan has covered up this true desire of his heart.
With the help of the Holy Spirit, we can discover what is our *real* wishes are and which *do not* correspond to God's will.
In this way we can become "our original" again. Like God has planned! For a detailed explanation see step 3/7 from p. 132. But look at it one after the other :-)
How did God discover the first sin, the cause of original sin? Adam and Eve were initially unaware that they were naked until they ate from the tree knowledge. Then they were ashamed and tied fig leaves on themselves. The consequences of this can still be seen today: Children have no problem playing andbathing naked together in the summer. Most adults are ashamed – an indication that we lost a lot of our childish intuition. This is reminiscent of the Bible passage when Jesus says in
Matthew 18,3 sagt: *"Truly I tell you, unless you change and **become like little children,** you will never enter the kingdom of heaven!"*

121

Hey guys – let's become like children, let's run to God like children full of trust in their beloved parents, let's have a good cry with Him. He's listening to us, wants to help us – we can't hide anything from Him anyway – and through our faith in His Son Jesus we receive eternal life with our ancestors and God in paradise!

The **Trinity** (this term does not exist in the Bible) is the unity of God (Father), God "as" Holy Spirit and Jesus, His Son.

Mary is neither part of the Trinity nor "Mother of God"! **God has no mother!** Mary was the mother of Jesus and a great role model for Christians. **But –** "**Holy Mary pray for us**"? Many Catholics pray that. If Maria heard this, she would say: "Why should I pray for you? Pray yourself and go to my son Jesus – why did I give birth to him? **Jesus can redeem you when you simply believe in Him and follow Him!**"

6.2 Do Christians Always Have to Go to Church? Never Having Sex Again?

The term church does not denote an old building that, smells like candles and incense and where old people sit and give a mean look at loud children. Nonsense! The etymological (= linguistic) source of the word "church" is the ancient Greek **ekklesia** and means "those who have been called out", i.e., those who believe in Jesus, who offer His good news, who serve people in love, who meet to praise God and much more.
"Church" is actually the *community* of people who believe in Jesus.

And what is "worship"? This is where believers thank and praise Him through songs sung and played together (usually at the beginning of a service). This may seem a little strange to outsiders, because – does God need to be "praised and worshiped"? *If* anyone knows that He is the greatest, then He is ... but it is also about us. Because in praise we can realign ourselves to God: For example, can I really, as the lyrics in some praise songs say, thank God for everything today? Forgive my neighbour? Love my spouse? Accept my life, as God has given me, with all its challenges? Find quiet? Pray? When we earnestly sing along to worship songs, we increase God's right to have access to our life, so that he can help us. Sure, God is omnipotent and He himself could get access to our lives

at any time. But He gave us free will and respects our decision – **we humans have responsibility about inviting God into our lives.**
Through the fall of man and original sin we live on earth, the fallen creation, in sin, *separated from God* – that is the real meaning of the term "sin" (see page 120). If God gives us faith in Jesus and we accept it, we are without sin before God – then He can bring our lives from the moment we turn to Jesus to full development or to repair it, for example we suddenly get to know the spouse of our dreams, get a job, make new friends, develop new talents and skills – but that's in the next chapter 6.3.

It's not about "going to church", it's also about finding support in a Christian community. There we get input and answers, especially for a successful start of our Christian life, edification and tips, how we can use our lifetime how Jesus would want it, overcome challenges with Jesus and share Jesus' love even in tricky situations. We get edification and an exchange of experiences, pastoral care, can serve our brothers and sisters in faith or can enjoy the fellowship with like-minded people and get knew strength. And what is ingenious and exciting: The common inquiry of God's word, the Bible, the most incomprehensible book of mankind – more exciting than the greatest adventure films, because now you are in the main role:

Expect the unexpected in your new life with God!

Never having sex again? Never having fun again? Nonsense! Being a Christian doesn't mean that from now on we have to roll our eyes and light candles with a self-pitying look and chastise ourselves. God gives us the ability to be joyful and have fun – also for sex! But within a marriage, see below. And yes, we do may also drink beer or wine. But ... everything with measure and aim, we should not become dependent on anything, but become free.

Sex is fun because God wanted it to be. And that makes sense too and the purpose of the matter, it's not just about reproduction, but also about the fact that a married couple can have a wonderful and (yeah! :-)) exciting experience together. But here, too, God created order, because ...

... Sex is something sacred – because it is our part in the act of creation!

Folks, *life itself* is behind this here!

Basically, there is no such thing as "sex before marriage" because in the moment when a couple sleeps together, they *are* married before God.
Genesis 2,24: *"That is why a man leaves his father and mother and is united to his wife, and they become **one flesh**."*
Even if a man "only" visits a prostitute for a moment, they become one flesh in God's eyes. Paul confirms this in
1 Corinthians 6,16: *"Do you not know that he who unites himself with a prostitute is one with her in body? For it is said, , '**The two will become one flesh**'."*

Important: To get to the point – according to the Bible, God does not want us to sleep around with multiple partners like rabbits ... cough, you know what is meant. The reason for that is,
If we lived our marriages according to the biblical recommendations, the fruits of this would be among others:
No sexually transmitted diseases.
Only desired pregnancies.
And the divorce rate would be exactly zero because there are only happy marriages. And this is how it works:

Whoever wants to live honestly with God (i.e., believes that is Jesus as the Son of God and their personal Saviour, obeys 10 commandments, forgives, loves people of different faiths and blesses, thus becoming a disciple of Jesus), **their life will be blessed by God:**
Which can also affect the fact that God can also bring us together with the love of our life (see also chap.6.3). In many Christian communities, marriages often take place at a young age because the couples received supernatural confirmation from God *and now know:* We are made for one another, there is a blessing over our marriage! And God blesses even abstinence of husband and wife during the engagement period, when they are saving their "first time" for the wedding night – it's much nicer then!
Your author tried it – no regrets!

But how will you get to know your dream partner? And know that "it's" him or her? Very simple: You will get supernatural affirmations from God for it, maybe you even become a prophetess or prophet – but how to do that is written in the next chapter:

6.3 How You Can Benefit from Jesus — Step by Step Instructions: Free Membership! Help for Everyone: Healing, Existence, Marriage and Much More The Greatest Time, Nerve and Energy Savings of your Life! The Greatest & Coolest Adventure! Safe through the End Times — Eternal Life in Paradise: how to get "into heaven"!

Preface — Step by Step Instructions Afterwards

"What do I need Jesus for? I'm a good person, I don't do anything bad!" This is a popular argument that we, the WithJesus-Team, have heard all too often. We answer these people: "Can you hear God?" The answer is usually "no". Explanation:

From chap. 2.2 it is proven that God lives.
But most of us cannot hear God.
This is the best evidence that this world, this earth, is in *a state of sin,* **and therefore is** *separate from God:* **a "fallen creation".**
Non-Christians live in a state of sin = separated from God.
(Christians are obliged to show mercy to them!)
Through our faith in Jesus, we come back in contact with God.
Anyone who becomes a Christian can claim all of the headings on this page for free. Please read heading 6.3 above again, paying close attention!

The whole thing about Jesus is so amazingly simple that some people can hardly believe it. In this way, a Hindu replied to the WithJesus-Team: "How should Jesus be able to redeem all of humanity? A good guru or master of Hinduism may be able to save five or seven people from a few reincarnations, but not all!" Nonsense! This can't be compared, **because it is our faith in Jesus through which the direct connection to God is restored, allowing God to make our lives blossom and to bring us to eternal life in paradise.**

From chapter 2.2 of this book it is proved that the prophecies confirm that ... God is alive.
That is why the rest of the Bible can be trusted. God wants it that way.
That is why God dictated the content of the Bible to the Jews.
For the good of *all people!*

The redeeming work of Jesus works according to this principle (this example is © WithJesus):
• Humanity screwed up and does it again and again.
• A *single*, let's call it "wrongdoing", has *a* consequence: *one*.
• A *thousand* wrongdoings have *a thousand* consequences: *a thousand*.
• Jesus committed *no* wrongdoing: *zero*.
• *But Jesus took the maximum consequence* to be taken: death on the cross.
• Someone has committed a thousand wrongdoings and becomes a Christian (= believes that Jesus God's Son, who redeemed us and sincerely repents), is therefore sinless:
• Because a *thousand* wrongdoings multiplied by *Jesus-zero* is: *zero consequences,*
• A *million* wrongdoings times multiplied by *Jesus-zero* is: *zero consequences,*
• a *trillion* misdeeds of *all people* multiplied by *Jesus-zero* is: *zero consequences.*

Everyone who sincerely repents of their wrongdoings and becomes a Christian, *because they believe* that Jesus died voluntarily on the cross paid for you = bought you free = accepted all the consequences, their bad deeds are "erased" before God, siehe
Colossians 2,14: *"He forgave us all our sins, having cancelled the charge of our legal indebtedness, which stood against us and condemned us; he has taken it away nailing it to the cross."*
These people come back in contact with God through their faith, invite Him into their life. God starts to repair our lives step by step and already saves us from sin *in our lifetime* = the separation from God and brings us to Him *after* our life = eternal life in paradise! (See chapter 2.7)

• All people who *do not* believe in Jesus and *do not* become Christians will be judged according to their works and conscience after death: Every person who does something that he / she *knows* is bad or forbidden, draws consequences to themselves: Curses like illness, loneliness, existential or other problems for themselves and for their descendants (!) – and might not go to heaven as easily (see chapter 5.3 "Hell" from p. 105).
Romans 2,12-16: *"Their **consciences** are also bearing witness, and their thoughts sometimes accusing them and at other times even defending them. This will take place on the day when God judges people's secrets through Jesus Christ, …".*
John 12,48 (quotation from Jesus!): *"There is a judge for the one who rejects me and does not accept my words; the very words I have spoken will condemn them at the last day."*

126

Revelation 20,13: *"... and each person was judged according to what they had done."* However, God's grace applies here too: A 10-year-old child soldier who is praised for shooting people probably won't have a bad conscience and is shaped, from a depth psychology perspective, by the fact that his horrific deeds are good – he has a chance for heaven.

But ...

... all people who *do not* believe in Jesus and *do not become* Christians, exclude God from their lives and don't give God the chance to help their lives, diminishing the chances of eternal life with God.

Imagine waiting for your execution on death row: the door is unlocked and opens; you think that is the end – and a completely perplexed security guard leads a guy into your cell who with a kind smile explains that HE wants to die for you! *Jesus has already done that for us!*

For all people who are *not* Christians, Jesus is a *judge*.
For all people who *are* Christians = believe in Jesus, Jesus is a *saviour*.

With Jesus you come into a freedom that you cannot imagine now.
John 8,36: *"So if the Son sets you free, you will be free indeed."*

This is also a huge opportunity:
Exodus 20,5: *"You shall not bow down to them or worship them; for I, the Lord your God, am a jealous God, punishing the children for the sin of the parents to the **third and fourth generation** of those who hate me, but showing love to a **thousand generations** of those who love me and keep my commandments!"* Das heißt:
1) When someone messes up, they are blocking God's blessing for themselves and their descendants – but God protects the descendants *starting from the great-grandchildren!* But ...
2) ... if someone becomes a Christian and seriously tries to follow Jesus by living a sanctified life – they will be blessed by God and thousands of generations of their descendants too!
Much greater than the consequences of excluding God from your life, is God's offer of blessings for you, dear readers!
Deuteronomy 7,9: *"Know therefore that the Lord your God is God; he is the faithful God, keeping his covenant of love **to a thousand generations** of those who love him and keep his commandments."*
Please turn the page, now things are getting exciting:

Do you want to receive the following things for free (it works, we promise!):
- Hear God?
- Solutions to your problems, such as fixing your marriage?
- Solutions to problems your family has (perhaps has had for generations)?
- Solutions to existential problems, e.g. a job that fulfils you?
- Get rid of illnesses? Get rid of addictions?
- Get to know your spouse?
- Get supernatural talents, such as becoming a prophet?
- Experience miracles?
- Or, let's assume the worst case scenario, you are rich, beautiful, happy, but still want the final adventure: To experience that God is alive?

Then it will be time for you to become a Christian:

Step I/7: Free Membership!

Now, that doesn't mean that God will make you and you a millionaire right away or will send you — for the purpose of starting a family — the hottest lifeguard or the sexiest underwear model.
God will first equip you to be able to deal with your new situation in life! Because, for example, countless poor lottery winners can't handle money, squander their win in no time and are poorer than before afterwards. In this way, God also prepares Christians personally for their development. You don't believe the above promises? Countless Christians have experienced all that and much more!

Whoever wants to come into contact with God personally accepts in faith,

- that Jesus is God's Son and our Savior because He voluntarily let himself be murdered on the cross for the purpose of extinction of the wrongdoings of all people who believe in it — He paid for you.
- that Jesus was buried in a cave after His death on the cross, that He was brought back to life by God three days later, has risen and shown himself to several people,
- and "follows Jesus", i.e., obey the 10 commandments, bless enemies and love, forgive, tell people about Jesus (you understand)

Important: no one can believe "on their own strength" or "on their own decision".

So ask the Holy Spirit first (that's God in His function as the Holy Spirit) that He gives you faith that Jesus is God's Son and has died for you.

Jesus explains this in
Matthew 16,15f: *"But what about you?' he asked. 'Who do you say I am?'*
Simon Peter answered: *'You are the Messiah, the Son of the living God!'*
Jesus replied: *'Blessed are you Simon son of Jonah, for this was not revealed to you by flesh and blood, but by Father in heaven!'"*

This is how easy prayer works in Christianity:
When people you love ask you something, do they need to remember to dress with dignity, celebrate incantation rituals or strange chants? No! Prayer is just as simple – you are allowed to come to God like a child to his loving parents. Jesus tells us that personally in
Matthew 6, 6-8: *"But when you pray, go into your room, close the door and pray to your Father, who is unseen. Then your Father, who sees what is done in secret, will reward you. And when you pray, do not keep babbling like pagans, for they think they will be heard because of their many words. Do not be like them, **for your Father knows what you need before you ask him!"***

This means that God knows, *before* we ask, not just what we *want,* but what we *need!* All too often these two things not the same.

You can't hide anything from God anyway. Even when you're angry, sad, exhausted or desperate: Scream, cry, pour your heart out in front of God (see chapter 2.3)!
This is Jesus' personal offer to us: *"Come to me, **all** you who are weary and burdened, and I will give you rest!"* (Matthew 11,28)

God hears you, comforts you, helps you and much more
Even if you have prayed honestly, you may feel that you have new faith right away, but only some time later. Consciously accept it. To let Jesus into your life, please pray the following prayer of surrender now.
Please turn the page ...

Step 2/7: The Prayer of Surrender

You are facing the greatest energy savings and the greatest adventure of your life: Becoming a Christian – you have the ticket in your hand.

Find a undisturbed, peaceful place of your choice where you feel comfortable. Either alone in the room or in a wonderful, beautiful landscape.
If necessary, at the toilet, it doesn't matter.
Ideally with someone you trust, as Jesus explains personally in
Matthew 18,19: *"Again, truly I tell you that if two of you on earth agree about anything they ask for, it will be done for them by my Father in heaven. For where two or three gather in my name, there am I with them."* **Wow:**
If two people ask something of God, He will give it to them! Of course, God will not grant the desire for a crime. But who prays together with another person, has a counterpart which warns them in case of stupid ideas arise.

Imagine that you are standing, sitting or lying in front of God personally – it's a little easier with your eyes closed. No, God is not ten feet tall old guy with a long white beard. *Just don't picture him.* That is what God likes best – because it makes no sense, because we cannot imagine God anyway. Even if you don't believe it now:
God, whom you may not see at the moment, now greets you with joy, goodness and love, with more than that your best friend or most loving parents who haven't seen their child in years and finally take it in their arms and show their heart! Fühlen Sie sich frei.
You can rest assured, because even if you don't believe it yet:

God is your Heavenly Dad, He hears you *now*.

Use the following lines as a **template** – you can say *everything* that is bothering you or what is important to you to God = Jesus. Talk to Jesus, who is one with God, simply in your own words:

"Dear Lord Jesus!
I believe that you died for my sins.
I believe that you are the Son of God,
that you died for me on the cross of Golgotha for my salvation,
that by doing this I am washed clean of all sin.

I put my old self (my 'old person') there on the cross,
please come into my life,
I believe that you will make a new person out of me!
I renounce all evil and its deeds.
Because you have forgiven me, I also want to forgive all people that have sinned
against me. Please God, in the name of your Son Jesus, help me with this.
Please strengthen and renew my faith!
Thank you that my name is in the book of life, that you are my Saviour,
please lead me into the truth, guide me into a free, developed and sanctified life
with your Holy Spirit!"

(Perhaps pause a little now, reflect, and ask the Holy Spirit to show you your wrongdoings. Meaning, everything that lies between you and your new life with God. For each of your offenses that the Holy Spirit has shown you, ask for forgiveness *in the name of Jesus Christ* and you will be forgiven instantly. Deleted, done, period. Yes, that corresponds to the Bible.)

"Lord Jesus – thank you for welcoming me now, forgiving me of all my sins., even
if I don't fully grasp it yet.
So, I also want to forgive all people, and I want to also forgive myself by trusting you.
I come to you, I give you my whole life, with all my worries, needs, problems, ill-
nesses, questions, with everything that burdens me, and I lay it down (this is now
meant symbolically, note) *before of your cross.*
And because you love me so much that you died for me, from now on I want to pass
on your love to the people around me in my life."

If you have said this prayer from an honest heart:
You are NOW at the beginning of a new life, *your* new life!

You have been forgiven by God for all your sins and you are *reborn in the Spirit of God!*
(No, that has nothing to do with re-incarnation, see chapter 4.2 of this book)

You are *now* God's child – Hurray!!! You can now feel like not a hero, but *in* an adventure film – expect the unexpected – from now on you live your life with God.
Our recommendation: Copy this prayer, write down the date and sign it, because it is the most important document of your life. Seriously.

Step 3/7: Find a Christian fellowship, be baptized

The term **church** does *not* refer *to* an old building that smells like candles and Frankincense but comes from the ancient Greek term **ekklesia** and denotes the *community* of believers in Jesus = the *"called out"*.

Find a Christian church. One where you feel comfortable – look at several churches. **Ask God for help, he will lead you into "your" church.** Yes, he can and will, even if this one thought may still seem completely impossible for you now. See chapter 2.3. Soon you will know which "your" church will be.

New Christians especially need fellowship – for a Christian it is a great refreshment to talk with another in "Christian language". Benefit from the many years of experience of seasoned Christians, listen to life testimonies, you will be very welcome! (And please be lenient if some Christians overwhelm you with tooooo many tips, in their excitement about their new sibling, namely you :-)).
In most communities, seminars are offered, the participation of which is almost is always free. For example, a so-called **alpha seminar,** a basic introduction to the Bible and to lived Christianity, with life testimonies and many exciting topics.

Or seminars on parts of the Bible, e.g. a letter from the Apostle Paul. Or on certain topics such as marriage, raising children, and much more In short, sharing about all areas of your new life with God.

A Christian community is important because it offers correction: Especially when you start being a Christian it can happen that you get lost in errors about Jesus and drift away from Him. Don't expect an ideal, perfect world – in Christian communities there is conflict since conflict exists wherever there are people. But we can admonish each other, learning from each other, "sharpening together".

Please be baptized. "What for?" We, the WithJesus-Team, often hear that. Or "I am already baptized"! In order: the baptism symbolizes death (immersion) and the resurrection, which proclaim new Christians not only to the "physical" world, but also, to the "spiritual" world, the otherworldly dimension, the "heavens", where God, angels and our ancestors live – yes, sorry, that sounds like a fairy tale, but read chap. 2.2-2.3. We can't see this dimension with our "carnal eyes", but sometimes God gives us a look inside. Many Christians have seen angels – perhaps you will too!

Especially in Free churches there is a party when people are baptized – but also in heaven there is jubilation when people decide for a life with Jesus!

Baptism is great because to be baptized you need *a certain attitude* **of the heart, a decision – and the** *inner* **attitude for it (less the external act) gives God the invitation into** *your* **life and the right to continue helping** *you* **in life.** John the Baptist explains in
Luke 3,16: *"I baptize you with water. But one who is more powerful than I will come, the straps of those sandals I am not worthy to untie. He will baptize you with the Holy Spirit and fire."*
Here John carries out the baptism with water, as the pastors do today. But God gives His Holy Spirit to it! This includes great gifts but more on that in in step 7.

Jesus was also baptized by John. But something happened during that, as told by **Matthew 3,16:** *"As soon as Jesus was baptized, he went up out of the water. At that moment heaven was opened, and he saw the Spirit of God descending like a dove and alighting on him. And a voice from heaven said:* **This is my Son, whom I love; with him I am well pleased!"**

The Spirit of God came upon Jesus *like* a dove – the Holy Spirit is *not* a dove, as painted in many churches. The Holy Spirit (= God *in His function* as Holy Spirit) is received by all people who decide to believe in Jesus, to follow him and to be baptized.

Then God also says to you: *"This is my beloved daughter / my son whom I love; with her / him I am well pleased!"*

A baptized person is born again – born again in Jesus: "the new Susan, the new Jimmy" – God starts to **make the baptized believers into an "original" from baptism onwards,** just as He originally intended. Liberated from past influences and injuries to life, which often have distorted people's personalities. For more information, see the paragraph on rebirth in Jesus & baptism in chap. 4.2 from p. 94.

"But I am already baptized!" WARNING: baptism is not baptism! The word baptism has its etymological (linguistic) origin in the Greek "baptizein", that means "immerse" or "submerge". An injection or Pouring water over a person to be baptized is *not* biblical baptism.

The **baptism of infants,** included in the Catholic Church among others, is a conflict-laden point of discussion within Christianity. **We from the WithJesus-Team believe the following: For example, A *blessing* of a small child would be logical; a baptism should only be done out of the free and independent decision by the person and at a point of appropriate maturity.** Regarding this, we, the WithJesus-Team, have a polite comparison with all due respect: Even a small child cannot drive a car, if you don't give them a driver's license ...

That is why we also recommend people who were baptized as children – usually just doused a little with water on the head – to catch up on the real baptism.

Step 4/7 - You can do this immediately:

- **Ask people with whom you are in conflict for forgiveness.**
- **Confess your new life with Jesus**

Now comes something you might not expect: Ask everyone in your life with whom you had any type of conflict, argument, dispute or something similar for forgiveness. Try to remove any kind of strife together with this person, making peace with each other through deep talk, which impacts both of your lives in a positive way. Should these people be missing or dead, then this can also work with a prayer. Forgive them, dismiss people from their faults in peace.

This is all about enabling you to start your new life with Jesus completely unburdened in peace and in freedom.

Perhaps it is also necessary that you meet someone you haven't seen in a long time and let this person throw accusations towards you during your meeting. It doesn't matter – alone your request for forgiveness because you have become Christian and want to start a life in peace with all people will already take the wind out of your opponents' sails – you will be amazed!

Confess your faith in Jesus – this is what Jesus personally recommends in **Matthew chapter 10, verse 32:** *"Whoever acknowledges me before others, I will also acknowledge before my Father in heaven!"*

Enjoy looking at completely perplexed faces: If your aunts and uncles talk about their last vacation, friends about their nights of partying or erotic adventures, colleagues about their newly acquired motorcycle, tell them just as casually that you have become a Christian. That will affect your relatives and acquaintances in such a non-conformative way that you know what real Rock'n'Roll is! :-)

Stick the notorious (:-)) Christian fish symbol on the back of your car. Und wenn dann Fragen von Nachbarn, Freunden, Familienmitgliedern auf Sie einprasseln wie von kleinen Kindern, warum Sie das getan haben, können Sie phantastisch gut die frohe Liebes-Botschaft von Jesus weitergeben.
Aber bitte nicht mit Zwang, überfordern Sie Ihre Mitmenschen nicht mit Ihrer Freude. Mehr Info später in Schritt 6/7.

The Christian fish is an ancient symbol, today a distinguishing feature especially for free church Christians. Many people stick a Christian fish on the back of their car. No, don't worry, nobody needs a harpoon because of that, as once recommended by the rock musician Frank Zappa.
The fish is said to have been a secret sign in times of Christian persecution: When two people met and they wanted to know: "Is the other Christian too?" both of them inconspicuously drew a bow with a stick of their foot in the ground (back then only a few paths were asphalted :-)). If the other one finished the bow, revealing the shape of a fish, then they knew: Wow, that's a sister or a brother in Jesus!
The fish logo is derived from two passages in the Bible. Here first the well-known passage where Jesus multiplied five slices of bread and two fish into a bountiful meal for a crowd of 5,000 people:
John 6, 1-15 (excerpt): *"Here is a boy with five small barley loaves and two small fish [...] they sat down ... about five thousand men were there ... Jesus took the loaves, gave thanks, and distributed to those who were seated as much as they wanted. He did the same with the fish. When **they had all had enough to eat ...** "*
Jesus' call for the creation of the fish logo is even more accurate:
Luke 5,10: *"Then Jesus said to Simon: ‚Don't be afraid; from now on you will fish for people.'"*

The letters of the Greek word for "fish", "I, CH, TH, Y, S" are the first letters of the creed: Jesus, Christ, God, Son, Redeemer. And Church Father Tertullian referred to Christians as "small fish" in AD 200. Please note: Fish live in water. Water is mostly a metaphor for the Holy Spirit in the New Testament. Christians live in the Holy Spirit – and they feel good, just like fish in the water! :-)

Step 5/7 – You can do this immediately:
• **Please start reading the Bible because ...**

... this book is incredible. Yes, there are several stories in the Old Testament about wars, but these are *always* fought brutally, even today.

But the Bible prepares you for all the future challenges for your life and holds miracles, healings, salvation and help, perspectives in store for you: How people hear the voice of God, are given a glimpse into heaven for free and much more! *For you!*

In his letter to the Ephesians, Paul describes the Bible as a *"Sword of the Spirit"*: **Ephesians 6, 17:** *"Take [...] the sword of the Spirit, which is the **word of God**."* "Sword" is meant metaphorically here because Jesus forbids violence! With your knowledge on the content of the Bible = sword of the Spirit, you can differentiate ("cut off") the bad from the good and orientate yourself in the general chaos. If someone tells you nonsense or wants to manipulate you, you will see this in comparison to the content of the Bible.

The important thing here is that you ask the Holy Spirit of God so that He reveals to you = brings to life the content of His word, the Bible!
A WithJesus-Staff wanted to read the Bible *before* he became a Christian but felt a strange blockage while reading. Only when he became a Christian did he understand the content of the Bible. Here is attempt to describe it: "Reading the Bible felt like I was trying to swim in honey. I just got stuck, the content and the words barely made sense to me, even though I was very interested and felt drawn to Jesus, something which I couldn't explain either. A couple of years later I became a Christian and suddenly I couldn't stop reading the Bible! I set my work aside, was unable to resist this book and read it for hours. While reading it was as if I could hear the sandals of the people in the Bible walking in the sand, as if I could hear their clothing swish while sitting right next to them!"

136

Don't give up – here is the solution: Ask God in your own words that He reveals His Word to you. Just like when you were a kid and asked your parents to read you something. Jesus confirms this in
Matthew 13,10f: *"Because the knowledge of the secrets of the kingdom has been given to you, but not to them. [...]* *"Though seeing, they do not see; though hearing, they do not hear or understand [...] For this people's heart has become calloused [...]* ***But blessed are you eyes because they see, and your ears because they hear.*** *"*
Start with the Gospel of Luke, then comes Acts – a dynamic story, as exciting as an adventure film!

Which translation of the Bible is recommended for whom? The **New International Reader's Version** Bible is written in English that is very easy to understand, also the **Contemporary English Version** (= 1995 revisited Good News Bible), the **The Living Bible** or the **New Living Translation**. The **King James Version** ist known for conservative English.
Written perhaps in a somewhat "awkward" English, but most precisely is sure to be the **New American Standard Bible (NASB)**.
No matter what translation: There is no point in keeping a valuable leather-bound Bible from 1820 on the shelf and letting it collect dust for decorative purposes.
Instead, it's better to have a cheap, messy school Bible in paperback, with a pea-green cover in the style of the 70s and to read it regularly.

Step 6/7: Following Jesus: Your Key

As always, there are a couple of commitments to be made. You can now for a long time talk on whether that is a "threatening message" or a "good news" – it's similar to traffic rules: If you run through a red light, you are in danger; drive when it turns green, and you are on the "safe side" – it comes to the same conclusion. **With the following system you give rights and an invitation to God to bring your life to unimaginable bloom, freedom and development.**

• Obey the 10 commandments – this will bring you protection & blessings
The Catholic Church has slightly changed their order and content.
You can find the original version in your Bible and here in
Exodus 20,1-17: *"I am the Lord your God, who brought you out of Egypt, out of the land of slavery.* **[1. Commandment]** *You shall have no other gods before*

137

me. [**2. Commandment**] *You shall not make for yourself an image in the form of anything in heaven above or on the earth beneath or in the waters below. You shall not bow down to them or worship them; for I, the Lord your God, am a jealous God, punishing the children for the sin of the parents to the third and fourth generation of those who hate me, but showing love to a thousand generations of those who love me and keep my commandments.* [**3. Commandment**] *You shall not misuse the name of the Lord your God, for the Lord will not hold anyone guiltless who misuses his name.* [**4. Commandment**] *Remember the Sabbath day by keeping it holy. Six days you shall labor and do all your work, but the seventh day is a sabbath to the Lord your God. On it you shall not do any work, neither you, nor your son or daughter, nor your male or female servant, nor your animals, nor any foreigner residing in your towns. For in six days the Lord made the heavens and the earth, the sea, and all that is in them, but he rested on the seventh day. Therefore the Lord blessed the Sabbath day and made it holy.* [**5. Commandment**] *Honor your father and your mother, so that you may live long in the land the Lord you God is giving you.* [**6. Commandment**] *You shall not murder.* [**7. Commandment**] *You shall not commit adultery.* [**8th. Commandment**] *You shall not steal.* [**9. Commandment**] *You shall not give false testimony against your neighbor.* [**10. Commandment**] *You shall not covet your neighbor's house. You shall not covet your neighbor's wife, or his male or female servant, his ox or donkey, or anything that belongs to your neighbor."*

• If you have sinned, do not sin anymore

No matter what sin you committed when you become a Christian, you will be forgiven, period. Yes, even with murder. Here is just one example of many in **Ephesians 4,28:** *"Anyone who has been stealing must steal no longer, but must work, doing something useful with their own hands, that they may have something to share with those in need."*

• Forgiveness instead of vengeance, blessing instead of curse: "Love your enemies!"

We know very well what people can do to other people. Also, what some Wannabe-Christians (because they weren't Christians!) did to other people, casts a shadow over the incredible message of love from Jesus. Even real Christians get thoughts of vengeance, but don't act on them – the life of Christians can sometimes be a real challenge!

God has forgiven us through Jesus, so we should also forgive people who have sinned on us, something which Jesus prays in the **Lord's Prayer** (Matthew 6: 9). **These are all quotes from Jesus personally in** (see next side)

Luke 6,37: *"Do not judge, and you will not be judged. Do not condemn, and you will not be condemned. Forgive, and you will be forgiven."*
Luke 6,27f: *"Love your enemies, do good to those who hate you, bless those who curse you, pray for those who mistreat you. If someone slaps you on one cheek, turn to them the other also. If someone takes your coat, do not withhold your shirt from them. Give to everyone who asks you, and if anyone takes what belongs to you, do not demand it back. Do to others as you would have them do to you. If you love those who love you, what credit is that to you? Even sinners love those who love them. And if you do good to those who are good to you, what credit is that to you? Even sinners do that. And if you lend to those from whom you expect repayment, what credit is that to you? Even sinners lend to sinners, expecting to be repaid in full. But love you enemies, do good to them, and lend to them without expecting to get anything back. Then your reward will be great, and you will be children of the Most High, because he is kind to the ungrateful and wicked."*

Do not take vengeance, God already says during the time of the Old Testament:
Deuteronomy 32,35: *"It is mine to avenge; I will repay."*
We are to forgive in trust, God will take care of the evildoer.

• Pay your "tithing" – this is how you can challenge God's blessing!
Pay your taxes on time, donate a tenth = 10% of your net earnings to the kingdom of Christ (Christian community, needy Christians, Christian ministries, etc.). *Not* 10% of gross earnings, because that's supposed to pay the tax Jesus explains in
Matthew 22,21: *"So give back to Caesar what is Caesar's* [note: the taxes]*, and to God what is God's* [note: tithing]*."*

God blesses us when we pay tithing – and with it (unique in the Bible!) we can even challenge God!
Malachi 3,10: *"Bring the whole tithe into the storehouse, that there may be food in my house. 'Test me in this' says the Lord Almighty 'and see if I will not throw open the floodgates of heaven and pour out* **so much blessing that there will not be room enough to store it!'"**

This is of course a test of trust: **the WithJesus-Team knows many Christians who have tried this practice of challenging God in times of existential need** – and they were brought out of their need by God! Suddenly a new job here,

139

a call with an offer of work, a gift there – God provides for those who trust in Him and follow his recommendations!

Your WithJesus-Author of *these lines* **has tried it out himself!** Indebted because he was betrayed, he still tithed, although not even 150% of his current money was enough to pay for the most urgent expenses: Food, electricity for his apartment, etc. Only two days, after he had done his first tithing, a wealthy Christian approached him and asked: "I got the impression from God, that I should lend you money!" The wealthy Christian could not have known anything about the plight of the betrayed brother – and lent him enough money so that he was able to obtain a debt restructuring. Everything continued upwards in giant steps: Orders flew into the house, customers paid reliably, he met a woman, started a family, paid off his home, became a WithJesus-Employee. An empirical-scientific proof: God provides for all people who trust Him – especially when they "tithe".

- **Remain true to the laws of your country, pray for bosses, politicians**
1 Timothy Kapitel 2,2: *"I urge, them, first of all, that petitions, prayers, intercession and thanksgiving be made for all people – for kings and all those in authority, that we may live peaceful and quiet lives in all godliness and holiness. This is good and pleases God our Saviour."*
Paul's letter to the Romans 13,1f: *"Let everyone be subject to the governing authorities [...] but also as a matter of conscience. This is also why you pay taxes."*
Yes, even if we like to get upset about superiors and politicians, our own leaders, or pastors of your own churches and maybe rightly so: Pray for these people, stay true to them – God has given responsibility to *these superiors.*
Exceptions:
1. in the case of requirements which go against Biblical principles. An extreme example for that: The obligation to betray and turn in Jews in Germany during World War II.
2. Or God tells you that you may leave your church because of inaccuracies or the like.

- **Be faithful in marriage.** Sex is great! But only within a marriage. Because basically there is no such thing as "sex before marriage", because *the moment* a couple sleeps together (even if the sex is paid for – if you understand), they are a married couple before God:
1 Corinthians 6,16: *"Do you not know that he who unites himself with a prostitute is one with her body? For it is said 'The two will become one flesh'."*

Sex is sacred – it is our part in the act of creation!
Folks, *life itself* is behind this!

Genesis 2,24: *"That is why a man leaves his father and mother and is united to his wife, and they become **one flesh**."*
Do you want maximum blessings? Then stay faithful to your spouse:
Matthew 5,27 & 28: *"You have heard that it was said, 'You shall not commit adultery.' But I tell you that anyone who looks at a woman lustfully has already committed adultery with her in his heart."*

Want to split up because you think your marriage is over? Nonsense!
Sorry guys – who do you believe in? **We're talking about the omnipotent God of the Bible, Father of Jesus Christ!** It is a piece of cake for God to give a couple their "first love" back! Sit down with your spouse and pray, Jesus recommends personally in
Matthew 18,19: *"Again, truly I tell you that if two of you on earth agree about anything they ask for, it will be done for them by my Father in heaven."*

• **Put the "Kingdom of God" first and foremost.**
Then God will provide you with everything you really need. The kingdom of God is the kingdom of Jesus' love & forgiveness. Putting it first means passing on love (also to enemies!), being compassionate & charitable, etc.
Matthew 6,33: *"But seek first his kingdom and his righteousness, and all these things will be given to you as well."*

Of course, this letting go is an act of trust: "I actually wanted to work and save money for my new car ..." But maybe we don't need a new car at all? Of course, we should work or take over responsibility in our families, but maybe God wants to, for example, protect us from unforeseen costs? The WithJesus-Team knows innumerable testimonies from Christian women and men who put their work on the kingdom of God above their prosperity: Suddenly a job with better pay came "out of nowhere" which also enabled them to have more time for their family and work for the kingdom of God. Or to have a sum of money to give support. Or God gifted Christians through completely unpredictable occurrences a house! Unrealistic?
Your WithJesus-Author of these lines is sitting in this house – now! Christians who seriously practiced this passage were healed from sicknesses, their marriages restored, their livelihoods saved.

• **Tell everyone about Jesus – and Jesus will stand in for you before God**
Mark 16,15: *"Go into all the world and preach the gospel to all creation. Whoever*
believes and is baptized will be saved, but whoever does not believe will be condemned [note: judged according to their conscience]. "

The last part of this statement from Jesus sounds brutal. But hell is a state rather
than a place. And people *themselves* cause this condition through rigidity and
pride – they reject the saving hand of God. This saving hand is God's offer to
believe in His Son Jesus.
This belief in Jesus is our guarantee for salvation and eternal life.

• **Tell about Jesus – but without compulsion, not like some intrusive mis-**
sionaries: This is what the prophet Zechariah (Old Testament) explains in
Zechariah Chapter 4, Vers 6: *"Not by might nor by power, but by my Spirit' says*
the Lord* Almighty. " [note: God is meant by this *] *"Not by might nor by power"*
means that you cannot convince people with the cleverest arguments – God
can only do this with His Holy Spirit. When some people (including people in
need that would actually need God's help) really want to hear nothing about
Jesus, follow Jesus' advice in
Mark 6,11: *"And if any place will not welcome you or listen to you, leave that place*
and shake the dust off your feet as a testimony against them. "
But you can and actually should always pray for those around you that they
accept the faith in Jesus in order to benefit immensely from it.

• **Pray – yes, it helps and works miracles! God hears you!** Whoever prays
gives God has the right to help in their life – more information in chap. 2.3.

Schritt 7/7 — Following Jesus: Your Wages!
Safe through the End Times. New skills.

Critics of Christianity denounce that "Christians give the responsibility of their
life to a God". Nonsense, that is not true – Christians take on *much more respon-*
sibility: Loving their enemies, offering their second cheek, practicing no retri-
bution or vengeance, always telling the truth, being merciful and much more.

In return, however, we are richly rewarded by God:
You will get talents = skills that you have never had before.

142

We know the "End Times" or the "Apocalypse" (Greek "unveiling") from numerous films which tackle "the end of the world", the third world war and similar inconveniences. Whoever reads the Bible carefully will discover that the End Times can only happen after the re-emergence of Israel (1948). So, we are getting closer and closer to that time.
But for this we are superbly equipped for God – here are further promises made by *Jesus personally:*

Are you worried? It works when you say to yourself "I don't want any worry – God will help me!" Pray to God in your own words because in
Matthew 7,7 (Jesus personally recommends): *"Ask and it will be given to you; seek and you will find; knock and the door will be opened to you!"*
Matthew 11,28 (offer from Jesus himself): *"Come to me, all who are weary and burdened, and I will give you rest."*

You give God more rights to help you when you pray with in a group of two or three people etc. – please read this incredible offer from Jesus in
Matthew 18,19: *"Again, truly I tell you that if two of you on earth agree about anything they ask for, it will be done for them by my Father in heaven. For where two or three gather in my name, there am I with them."*

Share your worries with Jesus in prayer. He will find solutions for you.
Matthew 6,25f: *"Therefore I tell you, do not worry about your life, what you will eat or drink; or about your body, what you will wear. Is not life more than food, and the body more than clothes? Look at the birds of the air; they do not sow or reap or store away in barns, and yet your heavenly Father feeds them. Are you not much more valuable than they? Can any one of you by worrying add a single hour to your life? And why do you worry about clothes? See how the flowers of the field grow. They do not labour or spin. Yet I tell you that not even Solomon in all his splendour was dressed like one of these. **If that is how God clothes the grass of the field, which is here today and tomorrow is thrown into the fire, will he not much more clothe you – you of little faith?"***
Matthew 6,33: *"But seek first his kingdom and righteousness, and **all these things will be given to you as well."*** (See Step 6/7)

Now that doesn't mean we can be lazy. We're supposed to do something – but God works in the background and there will be incredible, surprising incidents will happen – for your help.

143

Are you sick? Then pray for healing! Your belief in Jesus as the Son of God gives God the right to protect and heal you from all sorts of things:
Mark 16,18: *"They will pick up snakes with their hands; and when they drink deadly poison, it will not hurt them at all; they will **place their hands on sick people, and they will get well.**"*

If you have become a Christian, God will give you new talents!
God gives new abilities, also called anointing.
1 Corinthians 12,7: *"Now to each one of the **manifestation of the Spirit is given for the common good.** To one there is given through the Spirit a **message of wisdom,** to another a **message of knowledge** by means of the same Spirit, to another **faith** [note: f.ex.: to edify other people] by the same Spirit, to another **gifts of healing** by that one Spirit, to another **miraculous powers,** to another **prophecy,** to another **distinguishing between spirits,** to another **speaking in different kinds of tongues,** and to still another the interpretation of tongues. All these are the work of one and the **same Spirit,** and he distributes them to each one, just as he determines."*

You will get new skills: You can become a prophet, for example, you will suddenly practice a previously undiscovered talent of rhetoric (fluency), develop unimagined manual or intellectual skills, suddenly learn an instrument unusually quickly – all of these skills are needed in the kingdom of God.
Maintain = practice your new talents and they will grow!
Who is the Holy Spirit again? Info from page 118.

This is "speaking in tongues" also called "prayer in other languages":

It's a gift from God, "given" during one of **the most incredible occurrences of the Bible,** the so-called "Pentecost experience" = the first Pentecost, the **outpouring of the Holy Spirit** – here people for the first time experienced the Holy Spirit as the advocate announced by Jesus.

Please read Acts chapters 1 & 2 in your Bible.
More exciting than an adventure film because it *really* happened!

Explanation: The Holy Spirit inspired the young church of Jesus soon after his crucifixion and resurrection to do the so-called "speaking in tongues", and they have praised God with it. **Each of the new Christians heard the**

disciples of Jesus at that time suddenly speak in *their own* language! And the non-believers present could not explain this incredible miracle and thought that the Christians were drunk. Because "prayer in tongues" can sound a little strange or funny when you hear Christians (mainly in Free churches) pray with a concentrated face and closed eyes, loudly, softly, maybe singing, chattering, whispering, in their own languages with newly invented words. Or with words which exist in our languages, but still – for outsiders – are put together meaninglessly. But at some point, God gives every Christian who asks to be able to understand the prayer in tongues this ability. Speaking in tongues is a gift from God's Spirit, who communicates with our spirit – and it doesn't even matter whether the person praying can understand this exactly in the moment of prayer. Because while praying in tongues a person can express exactly what words can no longer express. A human, who prays "in new tongues" prays directly to God, Paul confirms.

Two practical examples of prayer in tongues or in tongues:

Example 1/2 A young Christian, new member of a Christian church, enters the service. They are singing worship and suddenly the whole church congregation begins to sing "in tongues". The young man hears this for the first time, is surprised at first, but then he understands what it is about – and for him the mix of tongues of the believers feels as if "heaven was open right above the church hall and as if thousands of angels are joining in the worship songs!". This is what the young, surprised Christian felt.

Example 2/2 A Christian woman, mother of a 14-year-old girl, is waiting in vain that the young teenager finally comes home after school at noon. As it gets later and later, the mother starts to have great fear – and suddenly begins to pray in tongues for the first time. "I didn't know what words I should pray because I was full of worry. But suddenly there were new words, a prayer flowing out of my mouth in a language unknown to me. It was as if I was praying away my fear with these new words!" The daughter came home safely shortly after that ...

• The Holy Spirit inspires us in the truest sense of the word (in spires = spirits "into us"), then we can – **including YOU, dear readers!** – prophesy, receive prophetic dreams, prophetic images & information from God – countless Christians have been able to experience that and that was confirmed to them in reality!

• Ask God to show you your new talents and your calling: Maybe you get the talent of prophecy, and suddenly learn supernaturally quickly learn to play an instrument or to sing (to praise God) or you become a brilliant organizer – the Bible is full of offers!

Safe Through the End Times. Do Not Worry!

If you become a Christian, then believe that Jesus is God's Son and died for us (more info see p. 118), God starts to repair our lives, helps them to come to full bloom and gives us supernatural talents and much more. But God also promises protection, because in the Bible wars and earthquakes are announced for the time before Jesus comes back.

Before the chaos starts, however, the Jews have to return to Israel – this was made possible with the revitalization of Israel in 1948.
Jeremiah 32,37 (600 BC): *"I* [note: God] *will surely gather them from all the lands where I banish them in my furious anger and great wrath; I will bring them back to this place* [note: Israel] *and let them live in safety."*

Even in difficult times: don't fear, but be happy, because ...
... God fights for us!
No matter if war, famine, pandemic, viruses strike – God will help us!

Hebrews 13,5-6: *"'Never will I* [note: quote from God] *leave you; never will I forsake you.' ... The Lord is my helper; I will not be afraid. What can mere mortals do to me?"*
Mark 13,7 (Jesus says): *"When you hear of wars and rumours of wars, do not be alarmed."*
Exodus 14,14: *"The Lord will fight for you; you need only to be still!"*
Matthew 5,12: *"Rejoice and be glad, because great is your reward in heaven."*

This is the "Rapture": If you are a Christian, you will be "raptured" before the rest of humanity goes nuts. Breathe deeply – with rapture nothing less is meant than that at a certain point in time all deceased Christians will be resurrected first in order to ascend to heaven with all living Christians worldwide afterwards, to meet the coming Jesus, who receives them in the clouds. All Christians will get to know their ancestors – if they were Christians too – even if they lived 200, 300 or 500 years ago. Hey, maybe you will get to know your devout great-great-great-great-aunt, who lived in the 14th century and that you never knew about before!

The Rapture *does not* mean the death of the believer, but a kind of supernatural evacuation before the chaos of the so-called "end times" hits. As crazy as this topic sounds, it is treated seriously in the Bible, so this should happen here too. In the original it sounds like this

1 Thessalonians 4,16: *"For the Lord himself will come down from heaven, with a loud command, with the voice of the archangel and with the trumpet call of God, and the dead in Christ will rise first. After that, we who are still alive and are left will be brought up together with them in the clouds to meet the Lord in the air. And so, we will be with the Lord forever."*

For this purpose, the earthly, i.e., "carnal" body, is transformed into a **"resurrection body"**, as Paul explains in

1 Corinthians 15, 44: *"It is sown a natural body; it is raised a spiritual body. If there is a natural body, there is also a **spiritual body** [...] in a flash, in the twinkling of an eye, **at the last trumpet** [...] the dead will be raised imperishable, and we will be changed."*

(More on the subject of the End Times can be found in the book "Believing? Knowing!" by the WithJesus-Team)

Yes, yes, strong stuff, we are aware of that – but God wants that we are doing well. And you can now, now, now start to claim it all.
For free!
So, if you haven't done so already ... go quickly to step 1/7!

7.0 Who Is the WithJesus-Team and What Do We Do?

7.1 We Are Not a Sect, but Normal People

"**WithJesus**" is an association of Christian artists, researchers, authors, musicians, historians, theologians and much more, who organize **events and concerts,** write **books, music** and **produce merchandise** (fan items such as printed t-shirts, caps, gifts etc). And all of that at the best price-performance ratio!

The unique and worldwide new thing about "WithJesus" is, however, that *nobody from our team* appears by their names: **We work anonymously, without fame or honour.** There are already enough "stars in the Christian arena". We have no Wannabe- CEOs, pseudo-bosses or self-appointed leaders, just people who shut up, get practical, and work.
Because only one person should get fame and honour: Jesus!

If you, dear reader, are *not* a Christian: This sentence may have sounded a bit pathetic right now; we are aware of that, however, the matter is explained in the book.
We are *not* aloof esotericists, End-Time prophets with clattering hand bells, whispering church goers, who look like they suffer, or people who light candles. We *don't* believe in UFOs that will bring Elvis back to us.

We are completely normal people who celebrate Christmas or with go on vacation with their families, build tree houses with the children, sometimes like to drink beer, or like to play with old cars. But God has given us exceptional talents that we want to pass on.
Our goal is:
1.) We want **everyone to have access to the greatest adventure this world** can offer and that is: to **become a Christian so that God can help.**
We organize great and fun evenings, with **live music, bands, encouraging talks and much more – with free entry or with an anonymous donation!**

148

And that without the messages filled with hidden occult, sex or hateful content and the like – nonsense, as it is common in today's music, for example.

Christian congregations of all denominations can "book" us and we organize a *free* evening event for them, which perhaps could become the most important and the most beautiful evening in a person's life. And it is attended by people who because of bad experiences or prejudices have stayed away from Christian events so far.

The WithJesus-Team wants to give *all* people (regardless of their origin or religion) real edification, hope and courage!

2.) We are working to bring all Christians of all denominations together so that Catholics, Protestants, Free Christians, Orthodox Christians and no matter what the Christians are called, **connect themselves again and find back to their one, only root: Jesus Christ, the Son of God.**
It's like bundling the light of a thousand small candles into a laser beam, which cuts the darkness!

We want to offer *everyone*, regardless of their belief, a new level of conversation!

When people (including Christians) learn to forget what separates them and to rediscover what connects them – then humanity can survive.
And what connects us is Jesus, who leads us with his incomprehensible deed to the path of peace, happiness, harmony, and a direct connection to God possible. You too, dear readers, can hear God. No, we don't eat drugs.

3.) Please subscribe to our videos on YouTube, visit our events, buy our books, music, fan articles. OUR GOAL: If you support our charitable work and God blesses us ...
... we want to finance residential projects which with cheap rents aim to help people in crisis situations or with existential problems to find a new start in a fulfilled life with unfolded talents.

PS.: And we aren't telling you about miracles in this book because we are Christians, but because we became Christians due to these miracles ... :-D

7.2 See you soon!

Of course, not all topics can be dealt with, or all questions can be answered in the 148 pages of this booklet. In the next books (including the book **"Believing? Knowing!"**) from the WithJesus-Team there will soon be hundreds of pages with much more additional exciting information and facts:
- Additional Evidence To the Uniqueness of the Bible, Including Archaeology
- Creationism vs. Theory of Evolution – what is fact, what is conspiracy
- That Is Why There Are Different Christian Currents
- This Is Exactly What the Bible Announces For the "End Times", This Has Come True So Far!
- This Is What the Biblical Prophecies Say About the Middle East Conflict
- The Facts Behind the Ominous "Protocols of the Elders of Zion"
- How to Use the Bible to Navigate the Babble Of Atheist Philosophies And the Jumble Of Esotericism and Occultism!
- How to Use the Bible to Uncover Conspiracy Theories!
- ... and much more!

None of the apostles gained any power of money through passing on the love message of Jesus. On the contrary: They just got more problems. **Stephen and Paul allowed themselves to be killed without resistance.**
And they forgave their murderers and blessed them.
They must have experienced something that was more important to them than their own life. **It was the miracles they experienced with Jesus Christ.**
 And the realization that Jesus is God's Son.

Important: we often hear, unfortunately mostly with a smug undertone, **"There are many spiritual ways – yours is the one with Jesus, mine is another one!"** as if real Christians want to force Jesus' message of love on someone. But real Christians don't do that, because that is impossible! That is why God also forbids this in the Bible, because only God's Spirit can reveal to people that Jesus is the Son of God is (see p. 140). God has a special path for every single person anyway and wants to spare us wrong ways that bring no fruit. **This book offers the most direct path to God for *all* people** (just as water is good for *all* who are thirsty) and with that offers the greatest savings of energy, nerves and time to enable us to lead a fulfilling life. **So that you too can experience that ... *God is alive!***
 God bless you all – see you soon!